GOTCHA Twice!

£16·95

£8.50

GOTCHA Twice!

The Art of the Billboard 2

Edited by Wei Yew

Published by Quon Editions © 1992

Printed in Singapore by Tien Wah Press

First Edition 1992

Quon Editions
#203, 10107 – 115 Street
Edmonton, Alberta
T5K 1T3 Canada.

Gotcha Twice! : the art of the billboard 2

Includes bibliographical references and index.

ISBN 0-9694432-9-3

1. Billboards. I. Yew, Wei, 1943-

HF5843.G67 1992 741.6'7 C92-090333-9

GOTCHA Twice!

The Art of the Billboard 2 *Edited by Wei Yew*

Quon Editions

Art Director
Wei Yew
Design & Production
Studio 3 Graphics
Printer
Tien Wah Press, Singapore

Contents

Since some of the billboards are quite specific in nature, the selected works are only roughly categorized in this contents page to facilitate quick reference and not intended as a definitive classification of billboards.

Preface

The billboard is a tremendous medium for getting attention, especially during an economic recession when the advertising dollar becomes precious. Since billboards cannot be switched off like television commercials, they have a potential to reach millions for the lowest cost per viewer. However, the billboard is also a difficult medium, for its cost effectiveness depends on its ability to deliver a message in mere seconds to someone travelling at 60 miles an hour.

Just shortly after the publication of *GOTCHA! The Art of the Billboard*, Tommy Teepell of the Outdoor Advertising Association of America called me about publishing a sequel volume. He suggested I include winners of the 50th anniversary (1992) OBIE Awards winners judged by Arnold Arlow, Penny Hawkey, Ray Jacobs, Bob Kuperman, Bob Kwait, Lee Lynch, and Ed McCabe. About 200 of these winners are featured in the first section of the publication.

GOTCHA Twice! The Art of the Billboard 2 also presents more of the best billboards submitted by advertising agencies and design studios from around the world. Works selected are again arranged here by subject, including public services; consumer products and services; entertainment, recreation and leisure; financial institution; newspapers; and many more.

A word of thanks to the following people for their assistance:

All the designers who took time to send in their works;

Tommy Teepell and Taylor Gregg of the OAAA;

John Bilney of Mediacom, Toronto for the introduction;

Yvonne McKinnon and Margaret Franklin, Mediacom;

Mary Yeow for organizing submission entries and tracking down the various resources.

Wei Yew

OAAA President's Message

This year marks the 50th OBIE Award Show, the opportunity we in the outdoor advertising industry take to recognize and thank a very select, elite few. These are the people whose creative talent insures the greatness of outdoor advertising; those whose efforts have brought them to the pinnacle of their profession. The winners of the OBIE awards, and eventually those taken into the OBIE Hall of Fame, have contributed a measure of themselves and their work that will stand as the benchmarks for those that follow.

Gordon Hughes III
President, Marketing
Outdoor Advertising Association of America

John Bilney is Vice President and Creative Director of Mediacom Inc., one of Canada's largest and most influential Outdoor Advertising companies. Prior to joining Mediacom in 1984, Bilney had been creative director at McCann-Erickson in Australia for two years, as well as MacLaren Advertising, Vickers & Benson in Toronto and J. Walter Thompson in Montreal. He has also owned his own film production company and has produced and/or directed over 1,000 TV commercials.

He has addressed advertising clubs in Atlanta, Memphis, Denver, Montreal, Vancouver and other cities, as well as making major presentations to large audiences of creative people. The titles of his presentations tell the story: 'Best of Britain' (1985), 'Frankly It's French' (1986), 'Hello Dali' (1987), 'Laughing On The Outside' (1988), and so on. His most recent presentation was at the Art Gallery of Ontario entitled 'Walking The Line', a plea for more creative latitude and daring on the part of advertisers.

Introduction

At Mediacom in Canada we spend a lot of time, talking to advertisers and ad agencies about ways to create for the Outdoor Media, showing them examples of great work from all over the world. I like to tell them that Outdoor Advertising companies should be out showing their customers how to use posters in ways that can bring fun, laughter and joy into peoples' lives. There's ample evidence that advertising which people like is more sales effective than advertising they don't like.

Much TV and Radio advertising seem to have been made under the assumption that consumers are completely lacking in intelligence, and herein lies an opportunity for Outdoor to outshine these other media.

I am often asked why the U.K. and French Outdoor is so good. My answer is that advertisers there seem to have less of a tendency to treat the consumer as a moron.

Don't misunderstand me. Canadian Outdoor at its best can hold its own with the best in the world, but it has been a long hard climb. The award winning posters in particular are intelligent, challenging and entertaining. And, yes, they are winning awards all over the world.

"But do they get results?" ask the marketing people. More often than not the answer is "Yes". Ask Levi's. Ask Evian Water. Ask McDonald's.

If you're reading this book, you're probably in the advertising business in some way, or at least related to it. I'd like you to stop thinking like an ad person for a minute and think of yourself as a 'consumer'. Because, of course, we are all consumers one way or another. We've got lives to live, we want to be amused, entertained and challenged. We don't want to be shouted at. We want to be coaxed and seduced.

Maybe Outdoor companies should point out to their clients that, in a strange way, they don't own the medium. The public owns it, because it is out in public and it can't be switched off. It should therefore be treated with great care. Advertisers simply must not waste or misuse space which belongs to all of us.

Maybe they should try to create more messages from the heart rather than the head. They could make their sisters laugh, disturb their brothers, make their mothers smile or maybe shed a tear, they could make their fathers jealous of their ability. There are so many ways to express oneself on a poster. Make people smile. Make them feel warm. Make them glad the ads are on the streets and in the buses and the subways. If you can do all that, yes, they might love you. Who knows, they might even buy your product.

One problem I see a lot of is the client who, on presenting a product to the creative team, also submits a lengthy product description. I have pleaded with the big packaged goods companies to learn to write a brief that's just that. Fifty pages of carefully considered verbiage can boggle the mind of a creative person producing a beautifully single-minded poster. I know what kind of advertising can result when a client simply hands over the product and says "Make me an ad." *Gotcha Twice!* contains a lot of ads that just might have been made in this way. I think they are the kind of ads all of us would like to see in Outdoor.

Excerpts from a speech he made recently to the 6th World Congress of Outdoor Advertising (1992) in Vienna.

BEST OF SHOW

Communications

Agency
Chiat/Day/Mojo
Art
Cabell Harris
Copy
Don Hughes

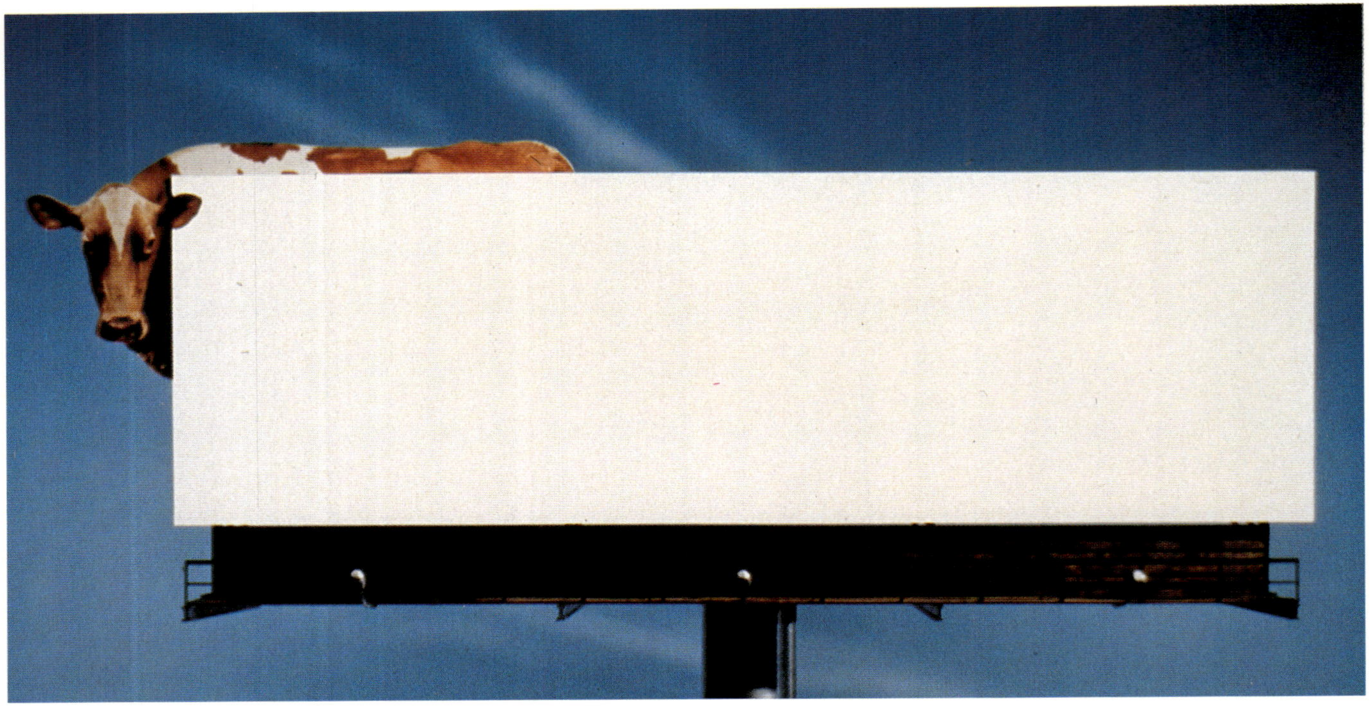

▸ Cowhides
If it's out there, it's in here.
NYNEX
Yellow Pages

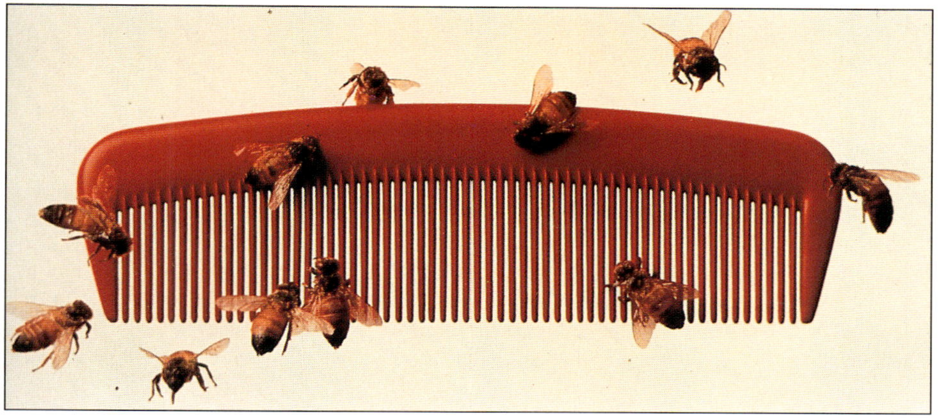

▸ Honeycomb
If it's out there, it's in here.
NYNEX
Yellow Pages

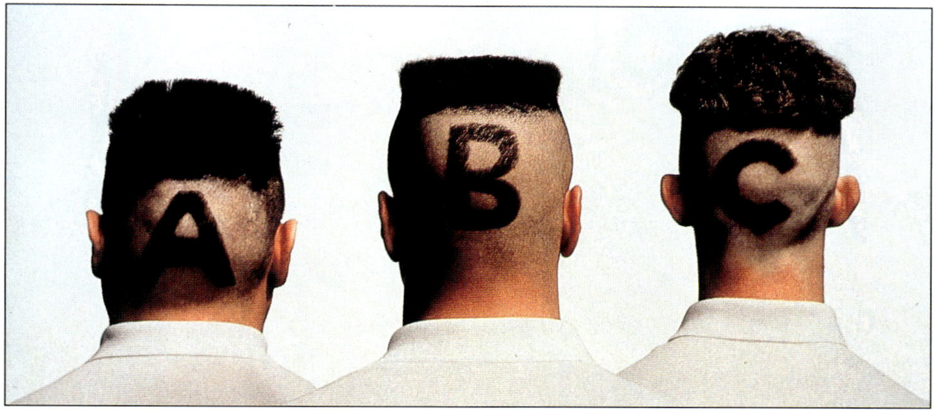
A
B
C

▸ Letterheads
A
B
C
If it's out there, it's in here.
NYNEX
Yellow Pages

BEST OF SHOW

Communications

Agency
Chiat/Day/Mojo
Art
Cabell Harris
Copy
Don Hughes

Hair Tinting
If it's out there, it's in here.
NYNEX
Yellow Pages

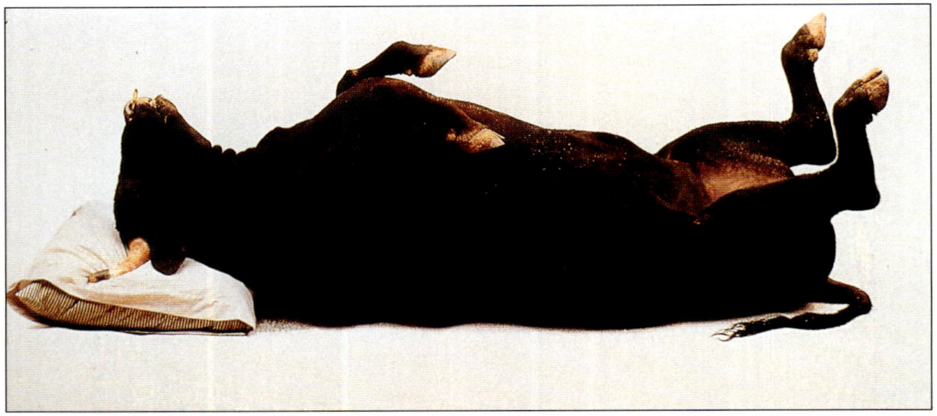

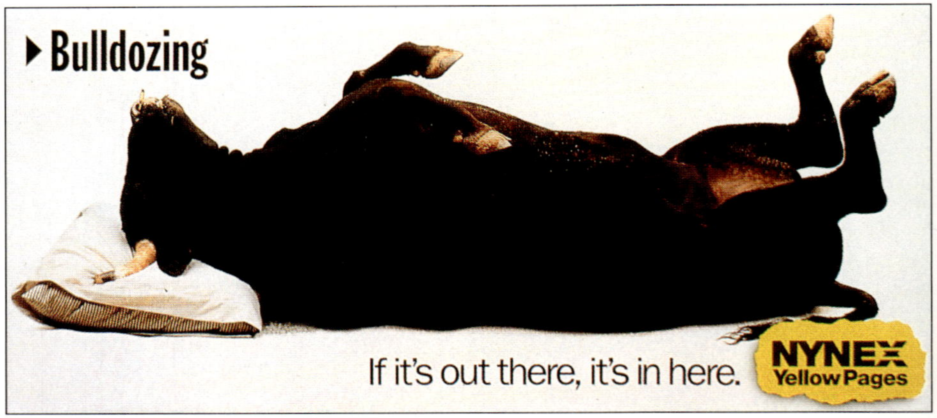
Bulldozing
If it's out there, it's in here.
NYNEX
Yellow Pages

BEST OF SHOW

Communications

Agency
Chiat/Day/Mojo
Art
Cabell Harris
Copy
Don Hughes

BUMBLE BEE
IN WATER
Chunk Light Tuna in Water
PICK UP THE TAB
FOR LUNCH.

OBIE AWARD

Food & Food Products

Agency
Phillips-Ramsey
Art
Bob Kwait
Copy
Joe Lazo

I'm Not Coming Down
Till First National Opens
A Branch in Green.

OBIE AWARD

Financial Products/ Services

Agency
Hitchcock Fleming & Associates
Art
Mark Collins
Copy
Jack Feeney

OBIE AWARD

Auto Aftermarket

Agency
Chiat/Day/Mojo, Inc.
Art
Jerry Gentile, Steve Diamant
Copy
Rob Feakins, Steve Rabosky

We also check your brake fluid.
QUAKER STATE
minit-lube
Reagan

We also work on boats.
QUAKER STATE
minit-lube

QUAKER STATE
minit-lube
Are you low on oil?

OBIE AWARD

Auto Aftermarket

Agency
Mitchell & Co.
Art
Joe Hemp, Flip Namur
Copy
Tom Hayes

OBIE AWARD

Clothing

Agency
Borders, Perrin & Norrander
Art
Terry Schneider
Copy
Greg Eiden

OBIE AWARD

Beverages

Agency
Grace & Rothschild
Art
Roy Grace, Don Miller
Copy
Diane Rothschild, Gary Cohen

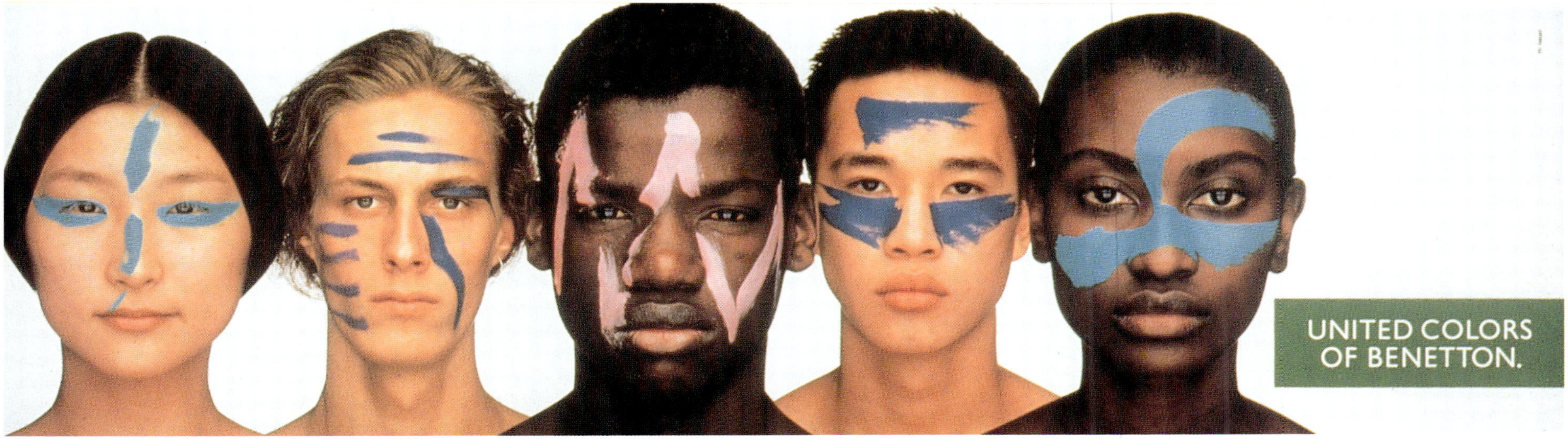

OBIE AWARD

Clothing & Accessories

Agency
Benetton Services Corp.
Art
Oliviero Toscani

Agency
Foote, Cone, & Belding - SF
Art
Craig Joslin, Keith Potter
Copy
Peter Angelos

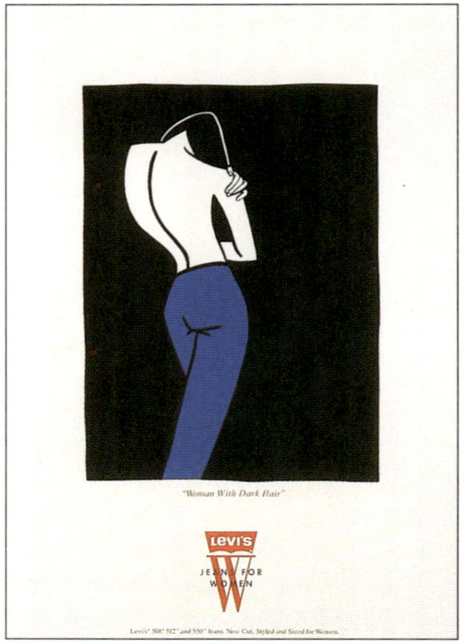

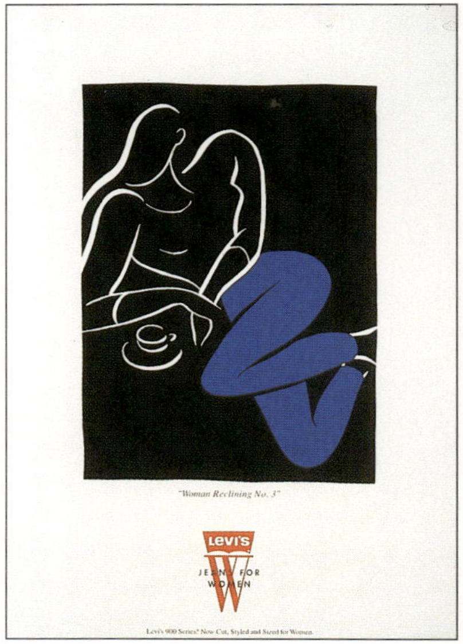

King-size bus poster (144" x 30")

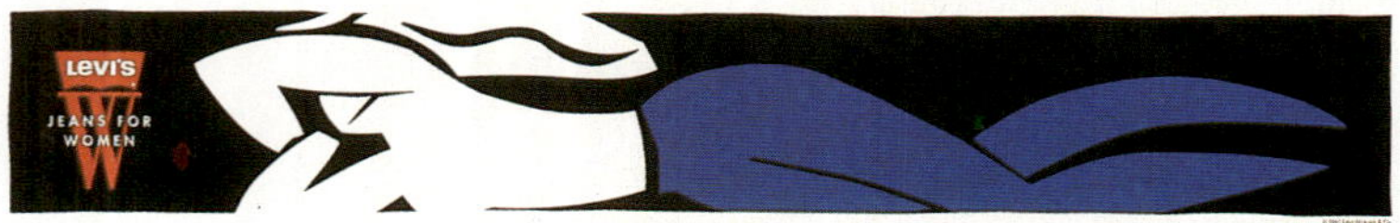

King-size bus poster (144" x 30")

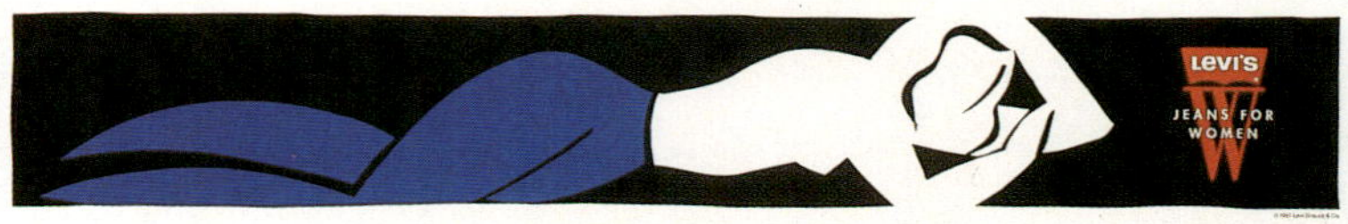

King-size bus poster (144" x 30")

Urban panels (60" x 30")

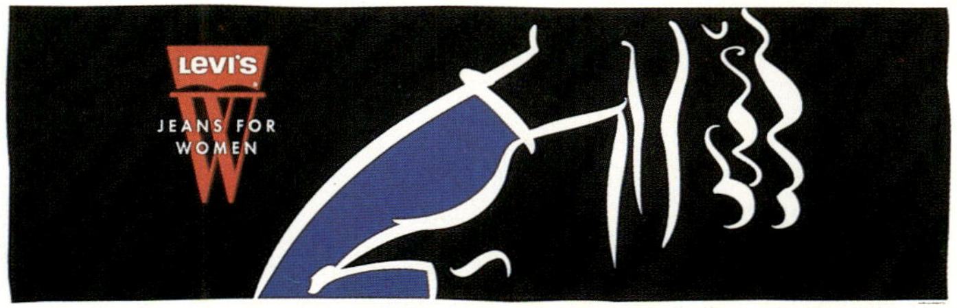

30-sheet posters (259" x 118")

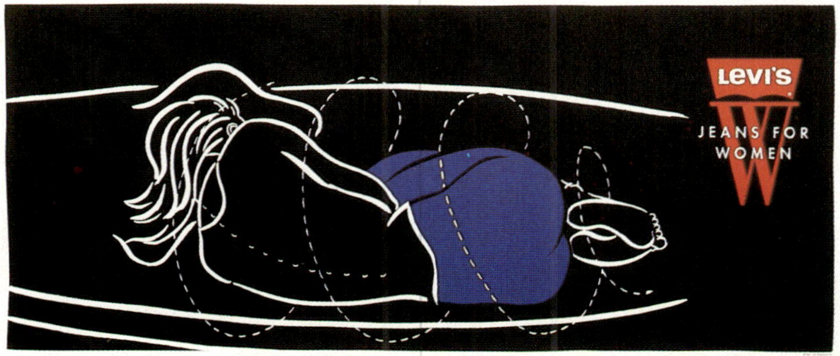

Urban panels (60" x 30")

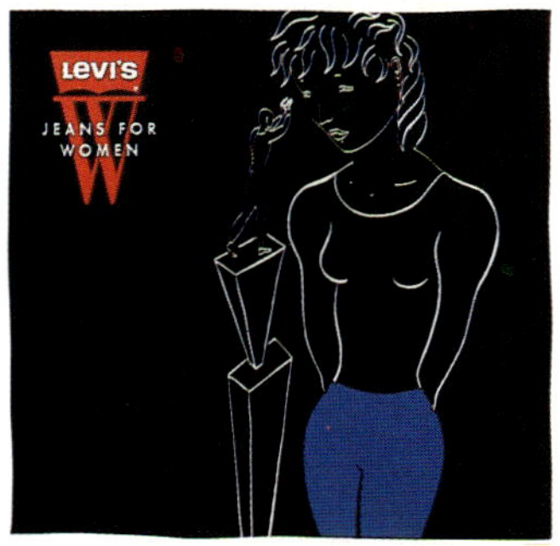

OBIE AWARD

Food & Food Products

Agency
Naegele Outdoor Advertising
Art
Al Appel
Copy
Tom Kocka

Campbell's
MINNESOTA'S "SOUPER BOWL"... ALL YEAR LONG.

BILLBOARDS DRAW PEOPLE LIKE FLIES.
Reagan

BILLBOARDS DRAW PEOPLE LIKE FLIES.
Reagan

BILLBOARDS DRAW
Reagan

DRAW
Reagan

OBIE AWARD

Media/Non-broadcast

Agency
Evans/Salt Lake City
Art
Steve Cardon
Copy
Bryan Deyoung

OBIE AWARD

Packaged Goods/HBA

Agency
Follis Devito Verde
Art
Tom Gianfagna, Rob Carducci, Abi Aron, Sal Devito
Copy
Sal Devito, Abi Aron, Rob Carducci, Tom Gianfagna

IT'S HARD TO KNOW IF YOU'RE EATING RIGHT, WHEN YOU DON'T KNOW WHAT YOU'RE EATING.
Solgar
It's A Tough Town. You Need A Tough Vitamin.

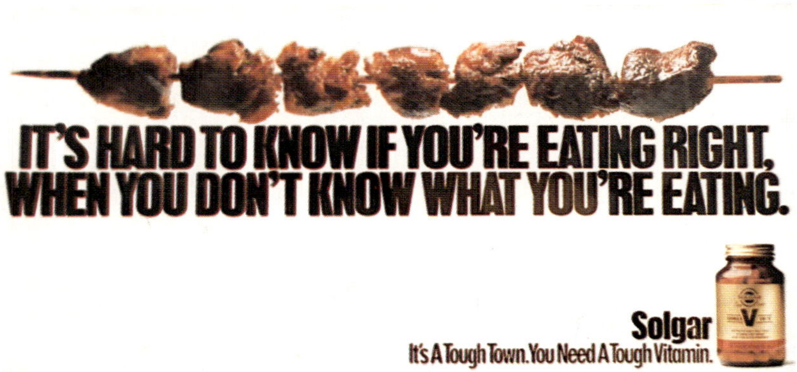
IT'S HARD TO KNOW IF YOU'RE EATING RIGHT, WHEN YOU DON'T KNOW WHAT YOU'RE EATING.
Solgar
It's A Tough Town. You Need A Tough Vitamin.

EVEN WITH EVERYTHING ON IT, THERE'S NOT MUCH IN IT.
Solgar
It's A Tough Town. You Need A Tough Vitamin.

FOR TOO MANY NEW YORKERS, THIS IS LUNCH.
Solgar
It's A Tough Town. You Need A Tough Vitamin.

New York Telephone
New York Telephone
FOR TOO MANY NEW YORKERS, THIS IS LUNCH.
Solgar

EVEN WITH EVERYTHING ON IT, THERE'S NOT MUCH IN IT.
Solgar

OBIE AWARD

Recreation/Spectator

Agency
Phillips-Ramsey
Art
Bob Kwait
Copy
Lynn Macey

Get on a roll.
Louisiana Downs
Racing Wed. thru Sun.

OBIE AWARD

Public Service

Agency
Evans/Salt Lake City
Art
Dick Brown
Copy
Dick Brown

Drunk Drivers
EXIT NOW
Gus Paulos
Chevrolet/Geo

OBIE AWARD

Public Service

Agency
Livingston & Company
Art
David Ayriss
Copy
Scott Vincent

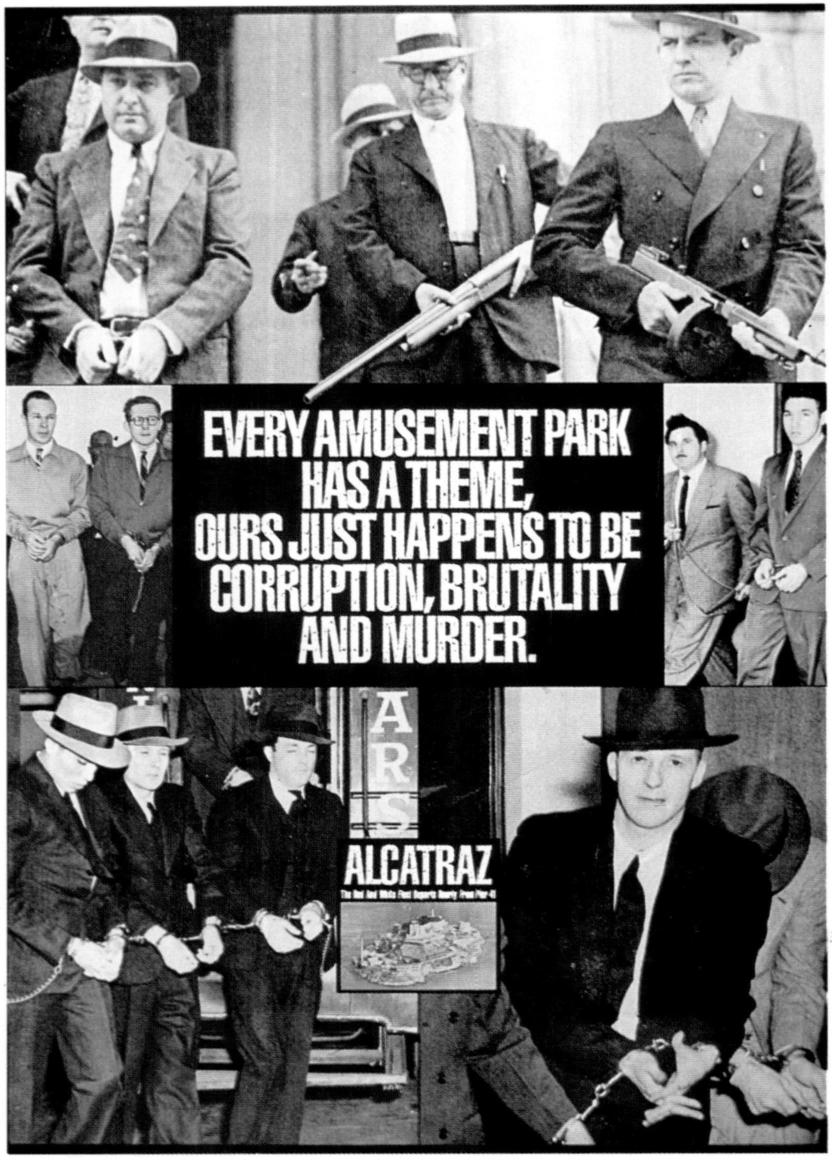
EVERY AMUSEMENT PARK
HAS A THEME,
OURS JUST HAPPENS TO BE
CORRUPTION, BRUTALITY
AND MURDER.
ALCATRAZ

IT MADE SING SING
LOOK LIKE BORA BORA.
ALCATRAZ

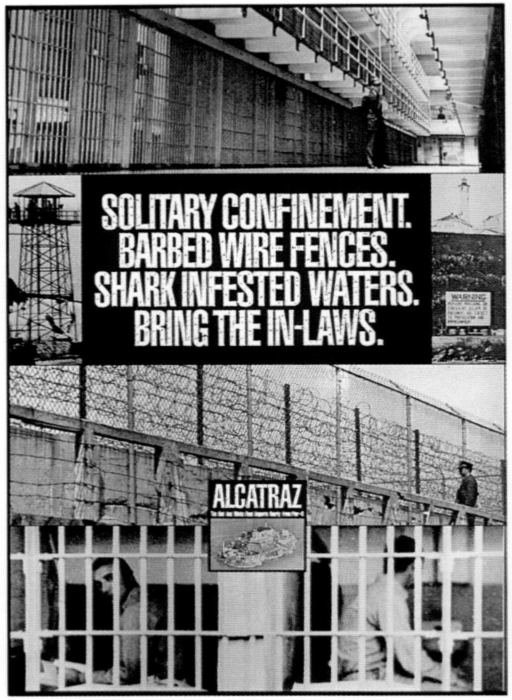
SOLITARY CONFINEMENT.
BARBED WIRE FENCES.
SHARK INFESTED WATERS.
BRING THE IN-LAWS.
ALCATRAZ

VISIT THE ORIGINAL
HARD ROCK CAFE.
ALCATRAZ

OBIE AWARD

Recreation/Spectator

Agency
Goldberg Moser O'Neill
Art
Michael Wilde
Copy
Jim Noble

WHAT 80% OFF ACTUALLY LOOKS LIKE.
Designer clothes 40-80% off.
DAFFY'S
GANNETT OUTDOOR

OBIE AWARD

Retail

Agency
Follis Devito Verdi
Art
Sal Devito
Copy
Sal Devito

Look so good, people will think you're shallow.
HORST
SALONS
NAEGELE

Make your ex-husband wish he weren't.
HORST
SALONS
NAEGELE

OBIE AWARD

Retail

Agency
Fallon McElligott
Art
Carol Henderson
Copy
Luke Sullivan

Dye yuppie scum.
HORST
SALONS
NAEGELE

Locks you won't dread.
HORST
SALONS
NAEGELE

Bow Wow.
HORST
SALONS
NAEGELE

Thairapy.
HORST
SALONS
NAEGELE

Your hair won't stand on end
unless you want it to.
HORST
SALONS
FAIRWAY

Incredibly, we're still exempt
from the luxury tax.
HORST
SALONS
NAEGELE

©1991 Horst Salons, Inc.
Our products are cruelty-free.
So are our haircuts.
HORST
SALONS

Before.
HORST
SALONS

Don't you hate it when this happens?
HORST
SALONS

What's wrong with this picture?
HORST
SALONS

OBIE AWARD

Retail

Agency
Fallon McElligott
Art
Carol Henderson
Copy
Luke Sullivan

WHICH DUMMY LOOKS SMARTER?
Designer clothing 40-70% off, every day.
5th Ave. & 18th St., Madison Ave. & 44th St.
DAFFY'S
$149
$550

WHAT 70% OFF ACTUALLY LOOKS LIKE.
Designer clothing 40-70% off, every day.
DAFFY'S

STANDING
ANY
IF YOU'RE PAYING OVER $100 FOR A DRESS SHIRT, MAY WE SUGGEST A JACKET TO GO WITH IT?
Designer clothing 40-70% off, every day. 5th Ave. & 18th St., Madison Ave. & 44th St.
DAFFY'S
CLOTHES THAT WILL MAKE YOU, NOT BREAK YOU.

OBIE AWARD

Retail

Agency
Follis/Devito/Verdi
Art
Sal Devito, Tom Gianfagna, Rob Carducci
Copy
Sal Devito, Tom Gianfagna, Rob Carducci

OBIE AWARD

Travel/Destination

Agency
BBDO
Art
Andy Weiskoff
Copy
Matt Branning

TAKE OFF, EH.
Alaska Airlines nonstop to Toronto.

ALASKA AIRLINES
TO SEATTLE.

GO BACK AND GET IT.
Alaska Airlines to San Francisco.
ACKERLEY

RAIN, RAIN. GO AWAY.
Alaska Airlines to San Diego.
ACKERLEY

TAKE ALASKA
AIRLINES TO L.A.

OBIE AWARD

Travel/Destination

Agency
Livingston & Company
Art
Matt Meyers
Copy
Dory Toft

OBIE AWARD

Travel Destination

Agency
Fotouhi Alonso Advertising
Art
Jorge Alonso
Copy
Farida Fotouhi

Tired of this?
Try this.
Palm Springs, CA 1(800) 34-Springs

OBIE AWARD

International

Agency
Harrod & Mirlin
Art
Graham Arnould

evian
MEDIACOM

Haven't seen you in a long, long, long, long time. Come to the Museum.
ROYAL ONTARIO MUSEUM

OBIE AWARD

International

Agency
Goeffrey B. Roche & Partners
Art
Geoffrey B. Roche
Copy
Jim Ranscombe

MERIT AWARD

Beverages

Agency
Frankenberry Laughlin & Constable
Art
Scotti Larson
Copy
Brad Berg

Da Chicago Beers.
Leinenkugel's
Original Premium Beer
Leinenkugel's
Limited
A Super Premium American Beer

MERIT AWARD

Automotive

Agency
Kresser/Craig
Art
Mark Rouse
Copy
Bob Satmary

Off the road again.
DAIHATSU

MERIT AWARD

Automotive

Agency
Rubin Postaer & Associates
Art
Bruce Bousman
Copy
Steve Chavez

You were always the smart one.
The Accord 4-Door
HONDA

KEEP
EVOLVING.
GANNETT OUTDOOR

KEEP
EVOLVING.
GANNETT OUTDOOR

KEEP
EVOLVING.
GANNETT OUTDOOR

KEEP
EVOLVING.
GANNETT OUTDOOR

KEEP
EVOLVING.
GANNETT OUTDOOR

KEEP
EVOLVING.
GANNETT OUTDOOR

KEEP
EVOLVING.
GANNETT OUTDOOR

KEEP
EVOLVING.
GANNETT OUTDOOR

MERIT AWARD

Beverages

Agency
Fallon McElligott
Art
Dean Hanson
Copy
Mike Gibbs

MERIT AWARD

Clothing Accessories/ Manufacturers

Agency
Hill Holiday Connors Cosmopulo
Art
Steve Tom
Copy
Mark Nardi

Hall of Fame Starter Kit.
THE PUMP™ Omni Zone II Basketball Shoe.
Reebok

MERIT AWARD

Financial Services

Agency
McCann Erickson
Art
Marlin Neuffeld
Copy
Michael Collins

DESIGNATE A DRIVER
WELLS FARGO BANK

MERIT AWARD

Media/Nonbroadcast

Agency
Franklin & Associates
Art
John Vitro
Copy
John Robertson

MOMMY, JASON SAYS PERESTROIKA IS A DOOMED IDEA. IS IT ?
THE TRIBUNE
FOR A SMARTER WORLD.

DADDY, CAN MY ALLOWANCE BE TIED TO THE CONSUMER PRICE INDEX ?
THE TRIBUNE
FOR A SMARTER WORLD.

MOMMY, WILL YOU EXPLAIN TRADE EMBARGOES BEFORE I GO TO BED ?
THE TRIBUNE
FOR A SMARTER WORLD.

The San Diego
Union

It will all make sense in the morning.

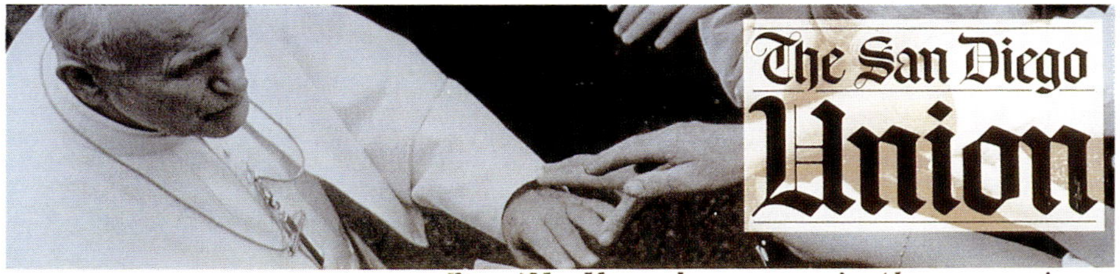
The San Diego
Union

It will all make sense in the morning.

The San Diego
Union

It will all make sense in the morning.

MERIT AWARD

Media/Non-broadcast

Agency
Franklin & Associates
Art
Mike Hall
Copy
Art Bradshaw

GUESS WHCH SCTN OF THE
PPER HS BN REDSGND?
The new, easier-to-use Star Tribune classifieds. Star Tribune
NAEGELE

NOW IT'S LSS DFFCLT
TO RD THE CLSSFDS.
The new, easier-to-use Star Tribune classifieds. Star Tribune
NAEGELE

CLSSFDS THT MKE IT ESIER
TO FND WHT Y'RE LKING FOR.
The new, easier-to-use Star Tribune classifieds. Star Tribune
NAEGELE

NWLY IMPRVD CLSSFDS.
The new easier-to-use Star Tribune classifieds. Star Tribune
NAEGELE

MERIT AWARD

Media/Non-broadcast

Agency
Fallon McElligott
Art
Carol Henderson
Copy
Doug de Grood

BLOW-BY-BLOW BASEBALL COVERAGE.
Star Tribune
NAEGELE

BLOCK-BY-BLOCK NFL COVERAGE.
Star Tribune
NAEGELE

MERIT AWARD

Media/Non-broadcast

Agency
Fallon McElligott
Art
Bob Brihn
Copy
Dean Buckhorn, Phil Hanft

WE WON'T LEAVE YOU HANGING.
Road to The Final Four.® Star Tribune
NAEGELE

Warning:
In Minnesota They Shoot Drunk Drivers.
Panasonic
MADD.
PAID FOR BY KARE
FAIRWAY

MERIT AWARD

Public Service

Agency
Clarity Coverdale Rueff Advertising
Art
Rob Dalton
Copy
Jerry Fury

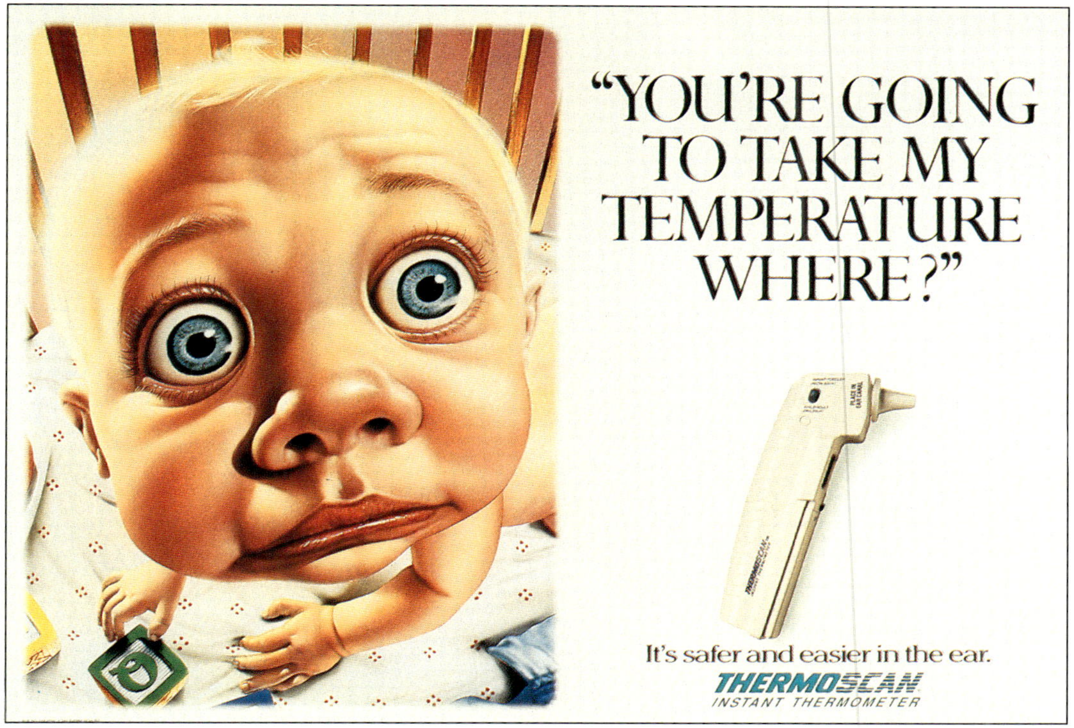
"YOU'RE GOING TO TAKE MY TEMPERATURE WHERE?"
It's safer and easier in the ear.
THERMOSCAN
INSTANT THERMOMETER

MERIT AWARD

Packaged Goods/HBA

Agency
Franklin & Associates
Art
John Vitro
Copy
Bob Kerstetter

EACH YEAR, OVER
1500 ELDERLY WOMEN
ARE RAPED.
MUST BE THE
PROVOCATIVE WAY
THEY DRESS.
Help stop the violence. Call 920-4642 for more information.
It shouldn't be a crime to be a woman.
The Violence Against Women Coalition

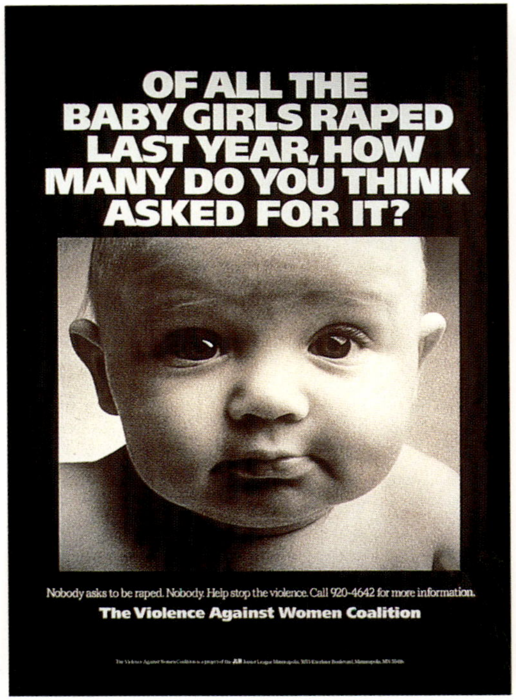
OF ALL THE
BABY GIRLS RAPED
LAST YEAR, HOW
MANY DO YOU THINK
ASKED FOR IT?
Nobody asks to be raped. Nobody. Help stop the violence. Call 920-4642 for more information.
The Violence Against Women Coalition

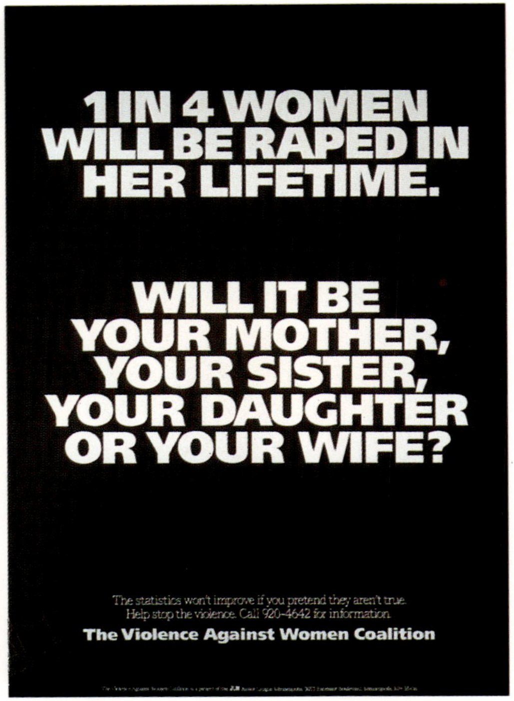
1 IN 4 WOMEN
WILL BE RAPED IN
HER LIFETIME.
WILL IT BE
YOUR MOTHER,
YOUR SISTER,
YOUR DAUGHTER
OR YOUR WIFE?
The statistics won't improve if you pretend they aren't true.
Help stop the violence. Call 920-4642 for information.
The Violence Against Women Coalition

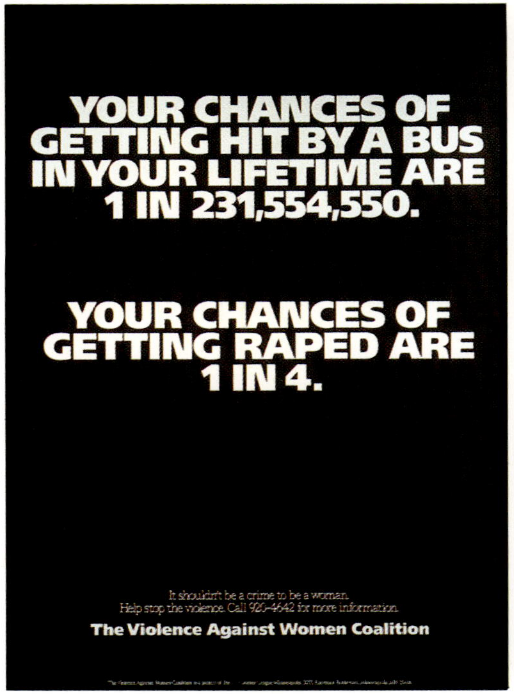
YOUR CHANCES OF
GETTING HIT BY A BUS
IN YOUR LIFETIME ARE
1 IN 231,554,550.
YOUR CHANCES OF
GETTING RAPED ARE
1 IN 4.
It shouldn't be a crime to be a woman.
Help stop the violence. Call 920-4642 for more information.
The Violence Against Women Coalition

A WOMAN
IS RAPED EVERY
SIX MINUTES.
UNFORTUNATELY,
YOUR BUS ISN'T
DUE FOR ANOTHER
FIFTEEN.
Rape is not a crime against just one woman. Rape is a crime against all women.
Help stop the violence. Call 920-4642 for more information.
The Violence Against Women Coalition

MERIT AWARD

Public Service

Agency
Fallon McElligott
Art
Carol Henderson
Copy
Bill Miller

DO CRACK WHEN YOU'RE PREGNANT, AND YOUR BABY DOES IT WITH YOU.
CRACK AND COCAINE CAN INJURE YOUR UNBORN CHILD FOR LIFE. OUR FOCUS PROGRAM CAN BE HEALTHY FOR BOTH OF YOU.
MODEL CITIES HEALTH CENTER
Call 222-6029 We'll help you quit.

DO COKE WHEN YOU'RE PREGNANT, AND YOUR BABY DOES IT WITH YOU.
COCAINE AND CRACK CAN INJURE YOUR UNBORN CHILD FOR LIFE. OUR FOCUS PROGRAM CAN BE HEALTHY FOR BOTH OF YOU.
MODEL CITIES HEALTH CENTER
Call 222-6029. We'll help you quit.

SMOKE WHEN YOU'RE PREGNANT, AND YOUR BABY SMOKES WITH YOU.
SMOKING CAN HAVE A VERY DANGEROUS EFFECT ON YOUR UNBORN CHILD. OUR FOCUS PROGRAM CAN BE HEALTHY FOR BOTH OF YOU.
MODEL CITIES HEALTH CENTER
Call 222-6029. We'll help you quit.

To Over 5,000
People In Madison,
This Is A
Mobile Home.
This bag is good for carrying around
a few belongings, but it makes a lousy pillow.
Help the homeless.

MERIT AWARD

Public Service

Agency
Lamaster Farmer Et Al
Art
John Walker
Copy
Jo Marshall

MERIT AWARD

Public Service

Agency
Lindsay Stone & Briggs Advertising
Art
Ron Brant
Copy
Ron Brant

MERIT AWARD

Recreation/Active

Agency
Chuck Ruhr Advertising
Art
Doug Dew

MERIT AWARD

Recreation/Spectator

Agency
Phillips-Ramsey
Art
Bob Kwait
Copy
Joe Lazo

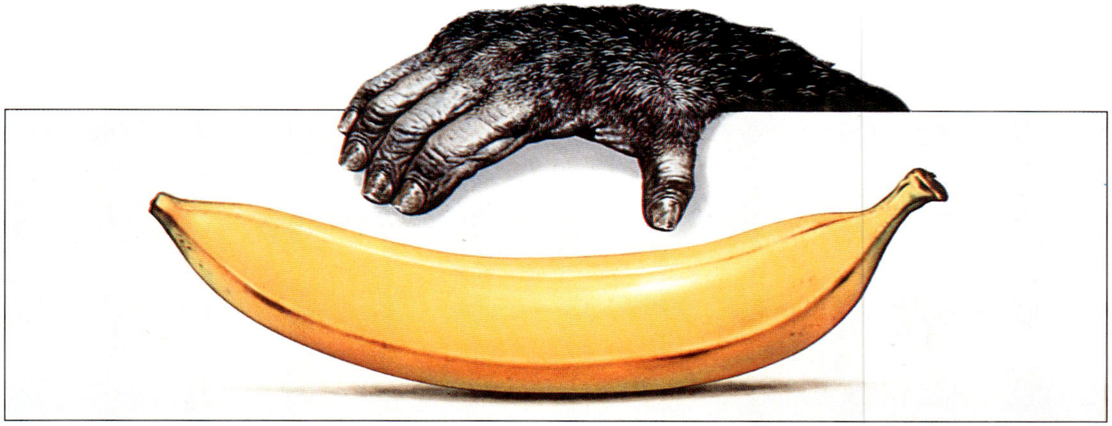

MERIT AWARD

Retail

Agency
The Puckett Group
Art
Scott Davis
Copy
Steve Puckett, Rich Wolchock

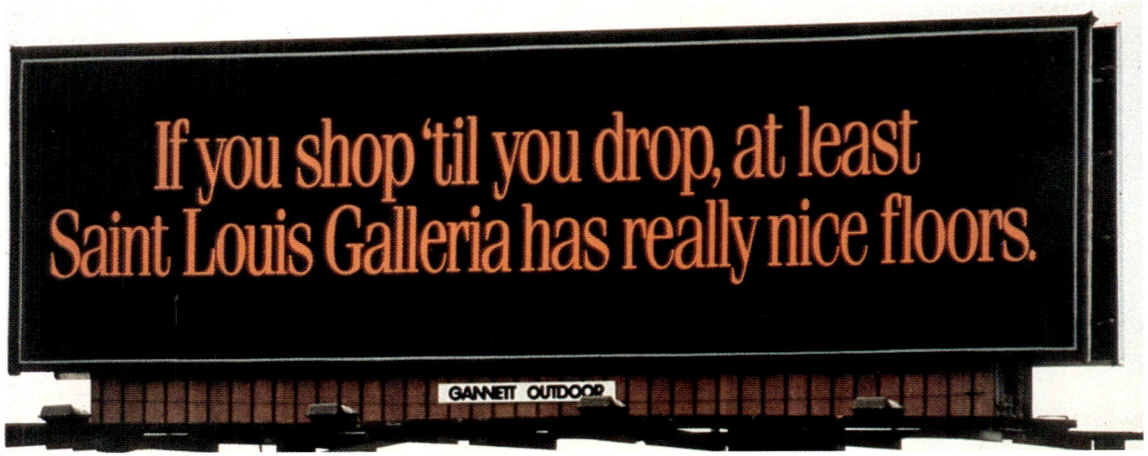
If you shop 'til you drop, at least
Saint Louis Galleria has really nice floors.
GANNETT OUTDOOR

If you spend money like there's no
tomorrow, we'd like to remind you that
Saint Louis Galleria is open today.
GANNETT OUTDOOR

If you're a compulsive shopper,
Saint Louis Galleria, Saint Louis Galleria, Saint L
Galleria, Saint Louis Galleria, Saint Louis Galler
GANNETT OUTDOOR

THE 6' x 6' BAYS YOU ORDERED ARE ONLY 5' x 5'.
THE CONCRETE LOAD WAS TWO YARDS SHORT. AND THE ARCHITECT SAID
HE WAS STOPPING BY WITH A FEW SMALL CHANGES.
STANLEY
STANLEY TOOLS

YOU HAVEN'T SEEN YOUR SHADOW SINCE MONDAY. BUT
THE BOARDS HAVE BEEN CUT. WHICH IS GOOD.
BECAUSE IF THIS KEEPS UP, YOU'LL NEED THEM FOR THE ARK.
STANLEY
STANLEY TOOLS

MERIT AWARD

Retail

Agency
Lawner Reingold Britton & Partners
Art
Dick Davis
Copy
David Abend

New York Telephone
A NYNEX Company
IN THIS NEIGHBORHOOD,
BE SURE TO KEEP
AN EYE ON YOUR WALLET.
Or shop at Daffy's 5th Ave. & 18th or Madison & 44th, and pay 40-70% less on designer clothing.

MERIT AWARD

Retail

Agency
Follis/Devito/Verdi
Art
Sal Devito, Ernest Neira
Copy
Sal Devito, Ernest Neira

V.P., G.M., C.E.O.,
A.S.A.P.
Apple
MEDIACOM
B.A., M.B.A., Ph.D.,
A.S.A.P.
Apple
MEDIACOM

MERIT AWARD

International

Agency
McKim/Baker Lovick/
BBDO, Toronto
Art
Jim Brown
Copy
Jim Brown

Just Think, To A Female Warthog,
This Is Tom Cruise.
METRO TORONTO ZOO
This summer's top gun. Sponsored by Procter & Gamble.

MERIT AWARD

International

Agency
Chiat/Day/Mojo
Toronto
Art
Duncan Milner
Copy
Joe Alexander

Knöw well.
Levi's
MEDIACOM

MERIT AWARD

International

Agency
Harrod & Mirlin
Toronto
Art
James Jung
Copy
Brent Peterson

IF YOU'RE NOT USING Clorets
YOU'RE WEARING YOUR BREATH.

IF YOU'RE NOT USING Clorets
YOU'RE WEARING YOUR BREATH.

MERIT AWARD

International

Agency
J. Walter Thompson
Toronto
Art
Marcee Ruby
Copy
Shelley Ambrose

MERIT AWARD

International

Agency
FCB/Ronalds-Reynolds
Toronto
Art
Barry Chemel
Copy
Elly Miller-Mostov

MEDIACOM
THE STREET HAS AN UGLY FACE.
COVENANT HOUSE
Life on the street is no life.

HELLP
There's a way out.
COVENANT HOUSE
Life on the street is no life.
COVENANT HOUSE. 70 GERRARD ST. EAST, 593-4849

ABUSES
Don't take it.
Take a bus
to Covenant House.
COVENANT HOUSE
Life on the street is no life.

A badly aimed sprinkler wastes water.
IT'S WORTH
SAVING
WATER

MERIT AWARD

International

Agency
DMB&B/Weekes Morris Osborn, Australia
Art
Michael Malherbe
Copy
Tim Brown

Ten dripping taps could fill this bus in less than six months.
IT'S WORTH
SAVING
WATER

WASH ME
IT'S WORTH
SAVING
WATER

MERIT AWARD

Miscellaneous

Agency
Wilson Horne McClelland & Gray
Art
Vynnie Meli
Copy
Pat Wages

"Atlanta Will Never Be A Baseball Town."
Provided by
ADAMS
Outdoor Advertising
ADAMS

FINAL

Beverages

Agency
DMB&B
Art
Bill Square
Copy
Bob Powers

Open Year Round.
Budweiser
KING OF BEERS
Bud
KING OF BEERS
Friends Know When To Say When

Good beer is properly aged.
You should be too.
Miller
NAEGELE

FINAL

Beverages

Agency
Frankenberry Laughlin & Constable
Art
Bill Kresse
Copy
Brad Berg

It keeps its head.
You should too.
Miller
NAEGELE

FINAL

Beverages

Agency
Frankenberry Laughlin & Constable
Art
Bill Kresse
Copy
Brad Berg

FINAL

Beverages

Agency
Grace & Rothschild
Art
Roy Grace, Don Miller
Copy
Diane Rothschild, Gary Cohen

Curling up with a J&B
patrick

Signaling for a J&B.
patrick

Basic Monday.
JIM BEAM
Basic Friday.

Basic Brooklyn.
JIM BEAM
Basic Manhattan.

Basic business.
JIM BEAM
Basic pleasure.

FINAL

Beverages

Agency
Fallon McElligott
Art
Bob Barrie
Copy
Jarl Olsen

FINAL

Beverages

Agency
Goodby Berlin & Silverstein
Art
Jeremy Postaer
Copy
Rob Bagot

FINLANDIA
VODKA OF FINLAND
Vodka From The Top Of The World.

FINAL

Beverages

Agency
Bauer Lein Inc.
Art
Ian Berry
Copy
Deunil Strickland

Thirsty?
10-K
THIRST QUENCHER
ADAMS

IN TEN YEARS THERE WILL BE 80,399,780 CATS ON THIS BILLBOARD.
Please Neuter Your Pets. HUMANE SOCIETY OF MISSOURI
3M National

FINAL

Public Service

Agency
Martin/Williams, Inc.
Art
Sally Wagner
Copy
Christopher Wilson

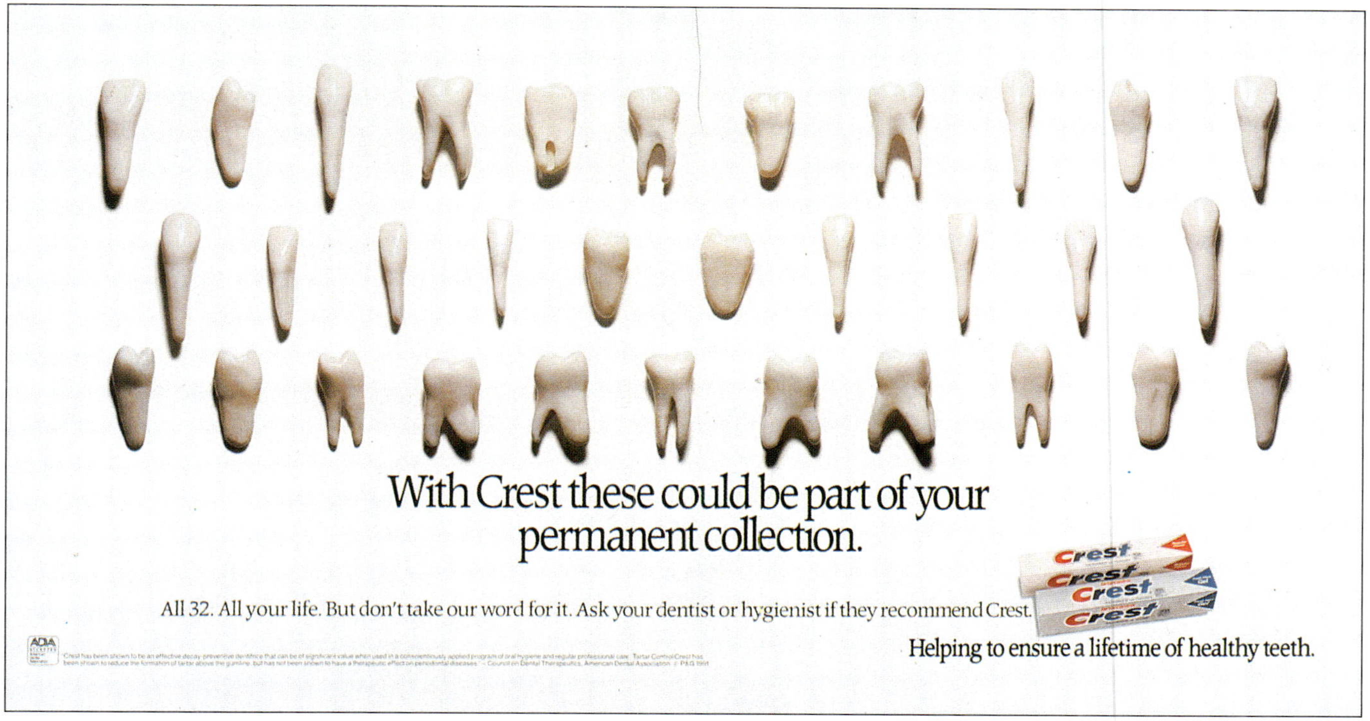
With Crest these could be part of your permanent collection.
All 32. All your life. But don't take our word for it. Ask your dentist or hygienist if they recommend Crest.
Helping to ensure a lifetime of healthy teeth.
Crest

FINAL

Packaged Goods/HBA

Agency
DMB&B
Art
Joe Staluppi
Copy
Yoni Mozeson

FINAL

Recreation/Spectator

Agency
Phillips-Ramsey
Art
Bob Kwait
Copy
Joe Lazo

Gorilla Tropics
Rain Forest
New at the San Diego Zoo

Gorilla Tropics
Peel off at the Pershing Dr. Exit.

TODAY, WE COULD SAVE THEIR NECKS.
Dinos to Rhinos Show
Wild Animal Park

ONCE AGAIN, HIS DAYS ARE NUMBERED.
Ends Oct. 4
Dinos to Rhinos
Wild Animal Park

SPINE TINGLING
Dinos to Rhinos Show
San Diego Wild Animal Park

On exhibit at
the Wild Animal Park
WHERE THE DEINONYCHUS AND THE EOBASILEUS PLAY.

FINAL

Recreation/Spectator

Agency
Phillips-Ramsey
Art
Bob Kwait
Copy
Joe Lazo, Bob Kwait

Every Day, We Start From Scratch.
Bashas'
OUTDOOR SYSTEMS

A Deli With The Works.
Bashas'
OUTDOOR SYSTEMS

FINAL

Retail

Agency
Crammer Krasselt
Phoenix
Art
Jamie Nichols-Hernandez
Copy
Jon Shore, Marianne
Curtis, Bruce Nilsson

The Choicest Choice.
Bashas'
OUTDOOR SYSTEMS

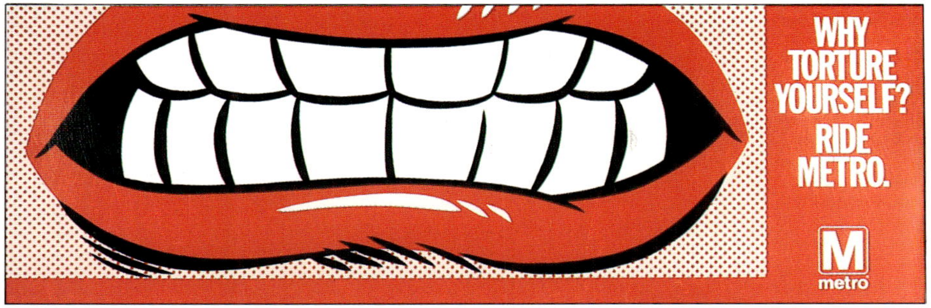
WHY TORTURE YOURSELF? RIDE METRO.
metro

WHY TORTURE YOURSELF? RIDE METRO.
metro

WHY TORTURE YOURSELF? RIDE METRO.
metro

FINAL

Travel/Transportation

Agency
Goldberg-Marchesano-Kohlman,Inc.
Art
Rich Park
Copy
Rich Park, Ed Stern

FINAL

International

Agency
Harrod & Mirlin
Toronto
Art
James Jung
Copy
Grahame Arnould

But the memories never fade.
Levi's

FINAL

International

Agency
Harrod & Mirlin
Toronto
Art
Mel McKelvie

MILK·BONE

DOMINOREOS
OREO

OREO
HUNKY-DUNKY-DOREO

FINAL

International

Agency
McCann-Erickson
Toronto
Art
Stephen Blair
Copy
Jeff Lewis

Keep a cool head.
CAB
STRAWBERRY

Australian Posters 3M
Keep a cool head.
CAB
CHOCOLATE

FINAL

International

Agency
Clemenger Brisbane Pty. Ltd., Australia
Art
Lyndon Harrison
Copy
Peter Goodall, David McClean

FINAL

International

Agency
MacLaren Lintas
Toronto
Art
Michael McLaughlin
Copy
Stephen Creet

A Sight
For Sore
Throats.
Bradosol
Bradosol Throat Lozenges.

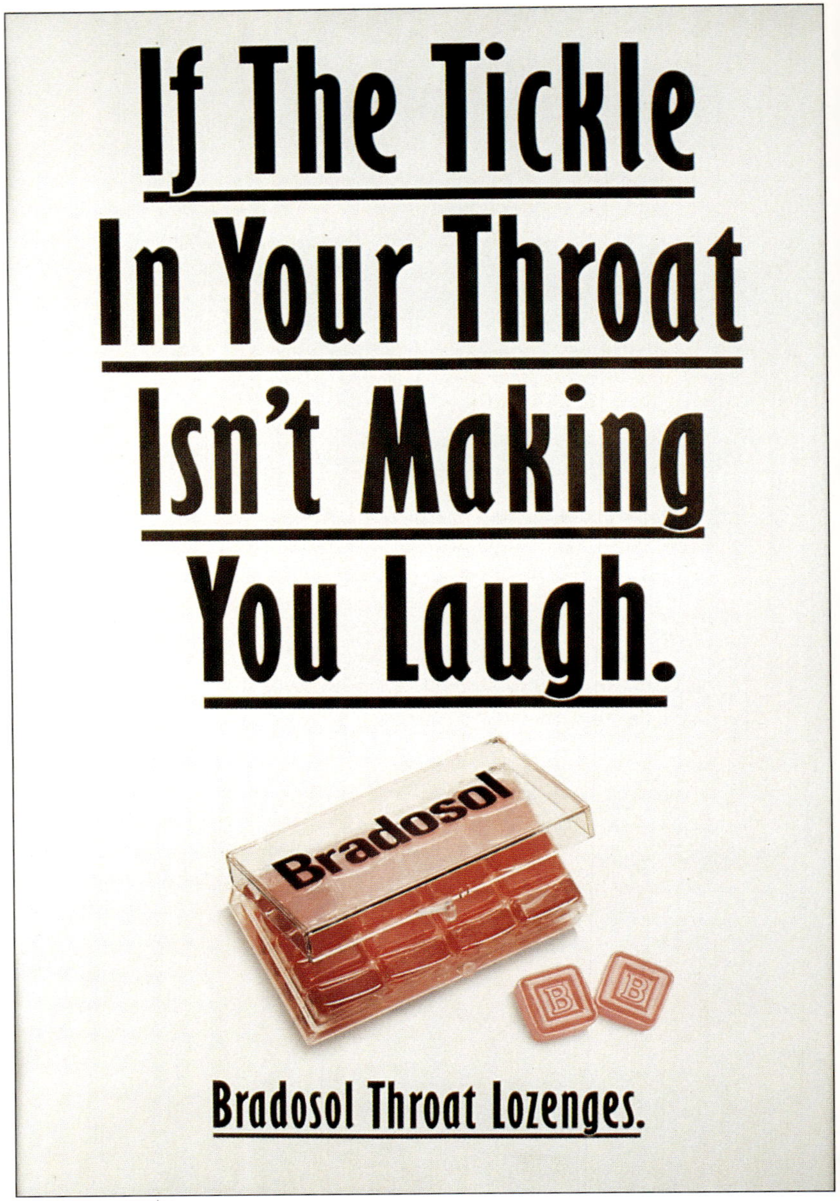
If The Tickle
In Your Throat
Isn't Making
You Laugh.
Bradosol
Bradosol Throat Lozenges.

Got A Frog
In Your Throat
Or A
Little Hoarse?
Bradosol
Bradosol Throat Lozenges.

It Goes
For The
Throat.
Extra Strength
Extra Fort
Bradosol

Bargain Hunting?
TARGET
RIGHT ON THE MONEY

Bargain Hunting?
TARGET
RIGHT ON THE MONEY

FINAL

Retail

Agency
Chuck Ruhr Advertising
Art
Randy Hughes, James Sansovich
Copy
Josh Denberg

Bargain Hunting?
TARGET
RIGHT ON THE MONEY

FINAL

International

Agency
The Gap (In House)
Art
Maggie Gross
Copy
Tim Cohrs

FINAL

International

Agency
Geoffrey B. Roche & Partners
Toronto
Art
Geoffrey B. Roche
Copy
Jim Ranscombe

In 850 B.C. she was
as popular as Madonna.
Come to the Museum.
THE ROYAL ONTARIO MUSEUM
WHAT'S ON AT THE ROM

Life before Nintendo Games.
Come to the Museum.
THE ROYAL ONTARIO MUSEUM
WHAT'S ON AT THE ROM

Bug your Parents
to come to the Museum.
THE ROYAL ONTARIO MUSEUM
WHAT'S ON AT THE ROM

Hang around
at the Museum.

Visit our
Suit Department.
Come to the Museum.
ROM Royal Ontario Museum

POMPADOREO
OREO
YOU'VE GOT TO ADOREO
AN OREO

DINOSOREO
OREO
YOU'VE GOT TO ADOREO
AN OREO

FINAL

International

Agency
McCann Erickson Advertising
Art
Stephen Blair
Copy
Jeff Lewis

PEOPLE READ
AS THEY GO BUY.
HOOK
Hook Outdoor Advertising. 483-3073
HOOK

Art Director/Designer
Chris Hamill
Design Agency
Hook Outdoor Advertising,
Edmonton
Copywriter
Chris Hamill
Client
Hook Outdoor Advertising

Advertise To People Who Are Going Somewhere.
Naegele Outdoor
NAEGELE

Hit 2 Million Moving Targets With A Single Shot.
Naegele Outdoor
NAEGELE

Art Director
Pam Mariutto
Design Agency
Martin/Williams Inc., Minneapolis
Copywriter
Tom Leydon
Client
Naegele Outdoor

Art Director
Steve Sweitzer
Copywriter
Jarl Olsen
Client
Ben Saltzman
Photography Inc.

Ben Saltzman
Photographer

MUST THEY FEND FOR THEMSELVES?
ISRAEL'S ELDERLY DEPEND
UPON YOUR RESPONSE.
Shaare Zedek Hospital

MUST THEY FEND FOR THEMSELVES?
ISRAEL'S CHILDREN DEPEND
UPON YOUR RESPONSE.
Shaare Zedek Hospital

Art Director/Designer
Jeff Layton
Design Agency
Jeff Layton & Assoc. Ltd. Toronto
Illustrator/Photographer
John Mastromonaco, Terry Pupplett
Copywriters
Sandy Silbert, Jeff Layton
Client
Canadian Shaare Zedek Hospital Foundation

Art Director/Designer
Jeff Layton
Design Agency
Jeff Layton & Assoc. Ltd., Toronto
Illustrator/Photographer
Ron Sehling, Terry Pupplett
Copywriters
Sandy Silbert, Jeff Layton
Client
Canadian Shaare Zedek Hospital Foundation

Part of you really wants
to stop drinking.
Options For Recovery
1-800-479-3339

Art Director/Designer
Bob Kwait
Design Agency
Phillips-Ramsey, San Diego
Photographer
Mike Balderas
Copywriter
Joe Lazo
Client
Child Abuse Prevention

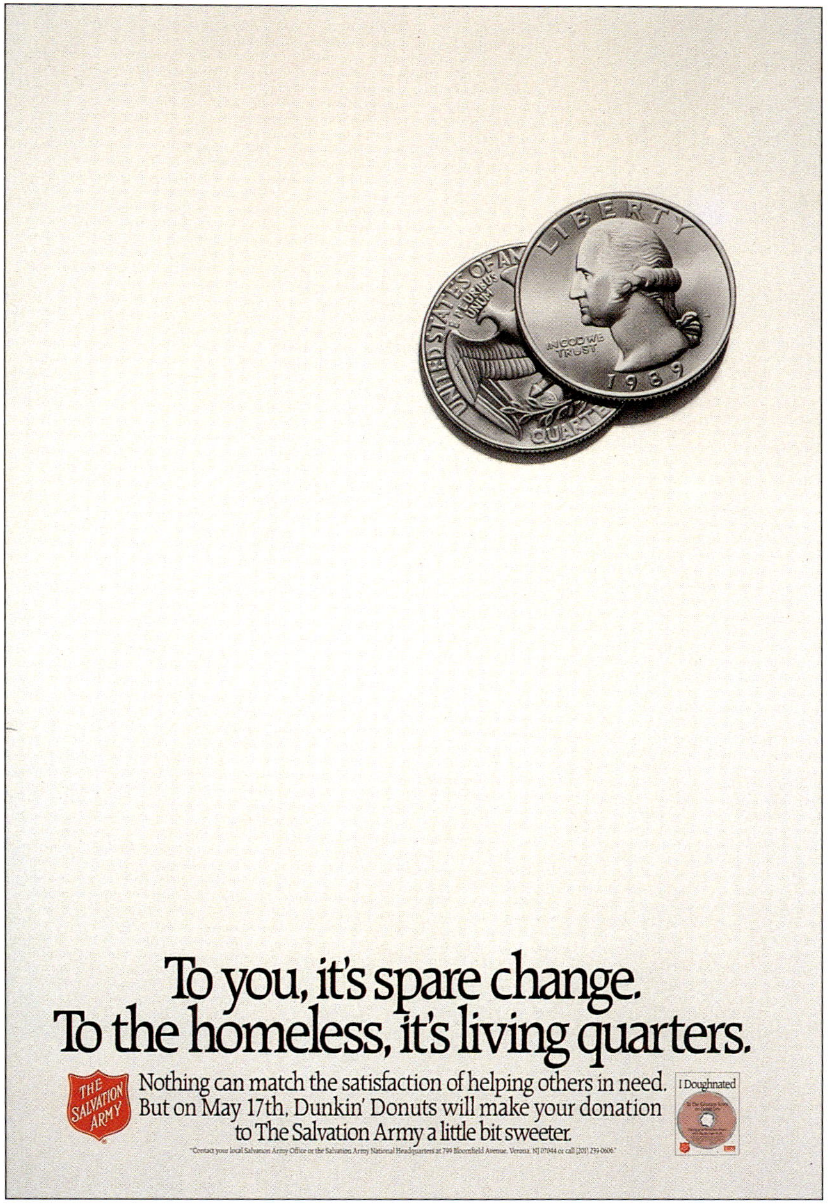
LIBERTY
IN GOD WE TRUST
1989
UNITED STATES OF AM
QUARTE
To you, it's spare change.
To the homeless, it's living quarters.
THE SALVATION ARMY
Nothing can match the satisfaction of helping others in need.
But on May 17th, Dunkin' Donuts will make your donation
to The Salvation Army a little bit sweeter.
I Doughnated

STAY IN SCHOOL
PITTSBURGH PUBLIC SCHOOLS OFFER NEW OPTIONS 622-3700

Art Director/Designer
Richard M. Seman
Design Agency
Seman Design Group, Pittsburgh
Illustrator
Richard M. Seman
Copywriter
Richard M. Seman
Client
Pittsburgh Public Schools

Art Directors
Mark Ware, Denise Emmerich
Design Agency
John Dough Advertising, Randolph
Copywriter
Bill Replogle

Creative Director
Jerry Green
Art Director
Roger Akerman
Design Agency
McCann-Erickson,
England
Photographer
Neil Mills
Copywriter
John Lewis
Client
Friends Of The Earth

THIS IS LITMUS PAPER.
WHEN ACID RAIN IS FALLING
YOU SHOULD SEE RED.
Friends of the Earth
THIS IS LITMUS PAPER.
THIS IS LITMUS PAPER.
THIS IS LITMUS PAPER.
WHEN ACID RAIN IS FALLING
YOU SHOULD SEE RED.
Friends of the Earth

If Kids Were All Alike, One Program Could Help Them All.
United Way

Creative Director
Bert Gardner
Art Director
Chris Lincoln
Design Agency
Bozell Inc., Minneapolis
Photographer
Tom Berthiaume
Copywriter
Dick Thomas
Client
United Way

THE THREE BIGGEST KILLERS IN AMERICA ARE CANCER, HEART DISEASE AND APATHY.
Please give generously.
United Way

Creative Director
Bert Gardner
Art Director
Chris Lincoln
Design Agency
Bozell Inc., Minneapolis
Copywriter
Dick Thomas
Client
United Way

Money Has A Way Of Changing People.
United Way
INVEST IN PEOPLE

Creative Director
Bert Gardner
Art Director
Steve Mitchell
Design Agency
Bozell Inc., Minneapolis
Copywriter
Doug Adkins
Client
United Way

Sweep the driveway instead
and save 150 gallons.
METROPOLITAN WATER DISTRICT OF SOUTHERN CALIFORNIA
WELLS FARGO BANK
GANNETT OUTDOOR

Turn the water off while brushing
and save 3 gallons
METROPOLITAN WATER DISTRICT OF SOUTHERN CALIFORNIA
WELLS FARGO BANK
GANNETT OUTDOOR

Art/Creative Director
Kathye Hicks
Design Agency
Eisaman, Johns & Laws,
Chicago
Copywriter
Ed Ball
Client
Wells Fargo Bank

Choose native plants and
save up to 1500 gallons a month.
METROPOLITAN WATER DISTRICT OF SOUTHERN CALIFORNIA
WELLS FARGO BANK
GANNETT OUTDOOR

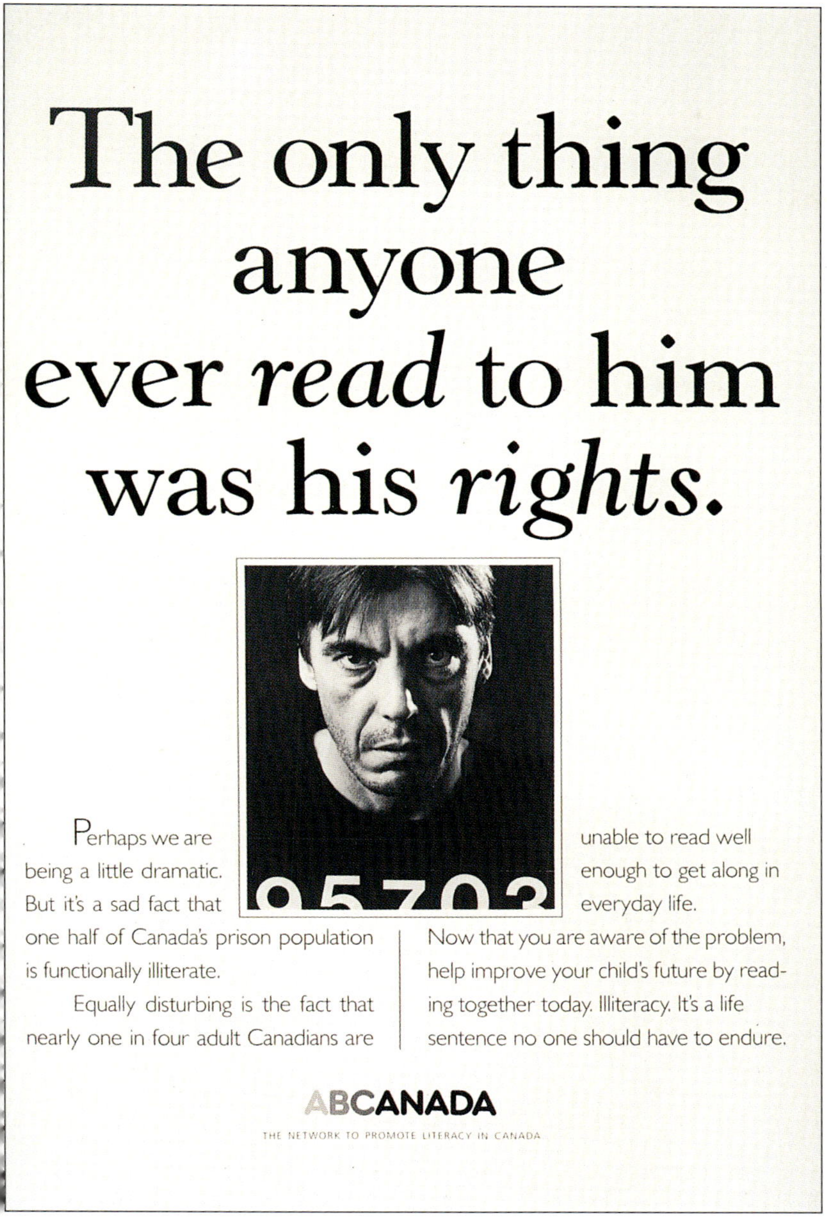
The only thing anyone ever *read* to him was his *rights.*
Perhaps we are being a little dramatic. But it's a sad fact that one half of Canada's prison population is functionally illiterate.
Equally disturbing is the fact that nearly one in four adult Canadians are unable to read well enough to get along in everyday life.
Now that you are aware of the problem, help improve your child's future by reading together today. Illiteracy. It's a life sentence no one should have to endure.
ABCANADA
THE NETWORK TO PROMOTE LITERACY IN CANADA

LEARN TO HOLD IT UNTIL YOU GET TO THE CAN.
DON'T LITTER.

Art Director/Designer
James Jung
Design Agency
Harrod & Mirlin, Toronto
Photographer
Bert Bell
Copywriter
Ashley O'Brien
Client
ABCANADA

Art Director
Patrick Arroff
Design Agency
DDB Needham, Los Angeles
Copywriter
Debbie Fried

NAEGELE
RECYCLE
Our
WORLD
MATTERS!
SPONSORE METRO SOLID WASTE AGENC

Art Director/Designer
John Sayles
Design Agency
Sayles Graphic Design,
Des Moines
Illustrator
John Sayles
Copywriter
Sheree Clark
Client
Des Moines Solid Waste
Agency

curbside
Recycling
WEDNESDAYS IN NORWALK
SPONSORED BY METRO SOLID WASTE AGENCY
NAEGELE

NAEGELE
OCTOBER 6
TOXIC WASTE
CLEAN UP DAY
METRO SOLID WASTE AGENCY 244-0021

We go to great lengths to help animals.
HUMANE SOCIETY
OF MISSOURI
3M National
004558

Creative Director
Lyle Wedemeyer
Art Director
Sally Wagner
Design Agency
Martin/Williams Inc.,
Minneapolis
Copywriter
Christopher Wilson
Client
Humane Society of
Missouri

Forget nine lives.
All a cat really wants
is one good one.
Adopt an animal.
HUMANE
SOCIETY OF
MISSOURI

Who says you
can't buy love?
Adopt an animal.
HUMANE
SOCIETY OF
MISSOURI

Single adults
make great
parents.
Adopt an animal.
HUMANE
SOCIETY OF
MISSOURI

Inside every puppy
a best friend is
waiting to happen.
Adopt an animal.
HUMANE
SOCIETY OF
MISSOURI

Art Director
Sally Wagner
Design Agency
Martin/Williams Inc.,
Minneapolis
Photographer
Kent Severson
Copywriter
Christopher Wilson
Client
Human Society of
Missouri

Many Americans still dine out!
SUPPORT
THE NATIONAL
URBAN LEAGUE

Art Director/Designer
Stephen Heckenbach
Design Agency
Whiteco Metrocom,
Merrillville
Photographer
John Beckett
Copywriter
Stephen Heckenbach
Client
R.J. Reynolds/The
National Urban League

Black and White together forever!
SUPPORT
THE NAACP

Art Director/Designer
Stephen Heckenbach
Design Agency
Whiteco Metrocom,
Merrillville
Photographer
John Beckett
Copywriter
Stephen Heckenbach
Client
R.J. Reynolds/NAACP

IF HE REALLY WANTS ATTENTION,
HE SHOULD JOIN OUR HEALTH PLAN.
TAKE CARE
THE CURE FOR THE COMMON HMO.
patrick

Art Director
Michael Wilde
Design Agency
Goldberg Moser O'Neill,
San Francisco
Copywriter
Jim Noble
Client
TakeCare Corporation

Creative Directors
Arnie Arlow, Peter Lubalin
Art Director
Geoff Hayes
Design Agency
TBWA Advertising Inc., New York
Photographer
Steve Steigman
Copywriter
Jeff Linder
Client
HIP

This way to the new YMCA.
It's just a short walk to 30 South Ninth St. Once you get there, ask for directions on how to get into great shape for just $29 a month.

Maybe it's not such a good idea to be all you can be.
If you think running an obstacle course means climbing over empty pizza boxes to change the channel, put yourself through basic training at the Y. Join for just $29 a month.
The New Downtown YMCA.
On 9th St. between Hennepin and LaSalle.

At rush hour, this is the sane lane.
Why hop into a car pool after work when you can jump into our eight-lane swimming pool instead?
The New Downtown YMCA
On 9th St. between Hennepin and LaSalle.

Creative Director
Jac Coverdale
Design Agency
Clarity Coverdale Rueff, Minneapolis
Photographer
Jim Arndt
Copywriter
Lee Schmidt
Client
YMCA of Minneapolis

It's next year.
Weight Watchers

Art Director
Fred Hooper
Design Agency
Stone, August, Baker Communications, Troy
Illustrator
Fred Hooper
Client
Weight Watchers

It's leap year
in Minnesota.
U.S. Olympic Festival-'90 July 6-15, 1990. Call Ticketmaster, 989-5151.

Catch a few butterflies this summer.
U.S. Olympic Festival '90 Call Ticketmaster 989-5151

Creative Director
Jac Coverdale
Design Agency
Clarity Coverdale Rueff, Minneapolis
Photographer
Paul J. Sutton
Copywriter
Joe Alexander
Client
U.S. Olympic Festival 1990

Creative Director
Jac Coverdale
Design Agency
Clarity Coverdale Rueff, Minneapolis
Photographer
Dan Helms
Copywriter
Joe Alexander
Client
U.S. Olympic Festival 1990

75¢
par jour*
* Transport inclus
Vidéotron
MEDIACOM

75¢
par jour*
* Tenue de jogging acceptée
Vidéotron

Design Agency
Tam-Tam inc. Publicité,
Montréal
Client
Videotron ltée

75¢
par jour*
*Adultes bienvenus
Vidéotron

75¢
par jour*
12
25
* Frigo à proximité
Vidéotron

75¢
par jour*
* Gardienne non requise
Vidéotron
consultez votre avocat!

Art Director/Designer
Steven John Wammack
Design Agency
Peter Hollingsworth & Assoc., Winston-Salem
Illustrator
Steven John Wammack
Client
SAFE Initiative (Substance Abuse Free Environment)

La collection du Musée,
c'est grandiose!
MUSÉE DU QUÉBEC
Ultramar
MEDIACOM

Creative Director
Yvon Brossard
Art Director
Benoit Pilon
Designer
Jean Lafrenière
Design Agency
Cossette Communication Marketing, Québec
Illustrator
Jean Lafrenière
Copywriters
Yvon Brossard, Benoit Pilon
Client
Museé du Québec

Creative Director
Pierre Audet
Art Director/Designer
Pierre Drouin
Design Agency
FOUG, Montréal
Illustrator
Tamara de Lempicka
Copywriter
Michel Lopez
Client
Montréal Museum of Fine Arts

Creative Director
Pierre Audet
Art Director/Designer
Pierre Drouin
Design Agency
FOUG, Montréal
Photographer
Michael Batchelor
Copywriter
Michel Lopez
Client
Montréal Museum of Fine Arts

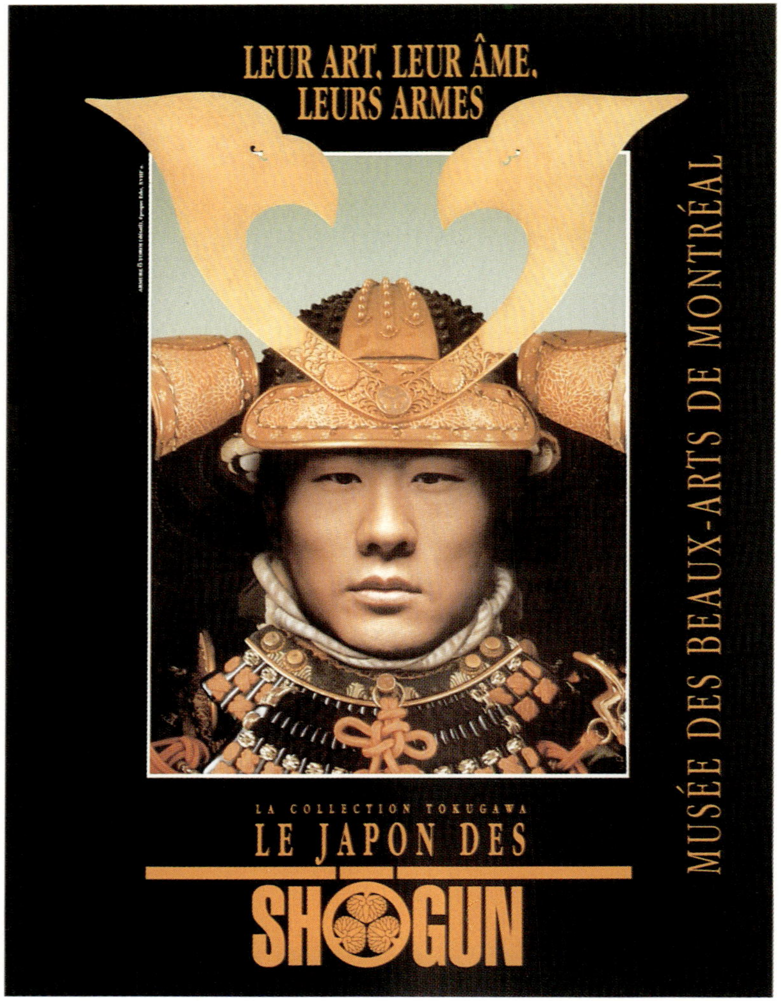

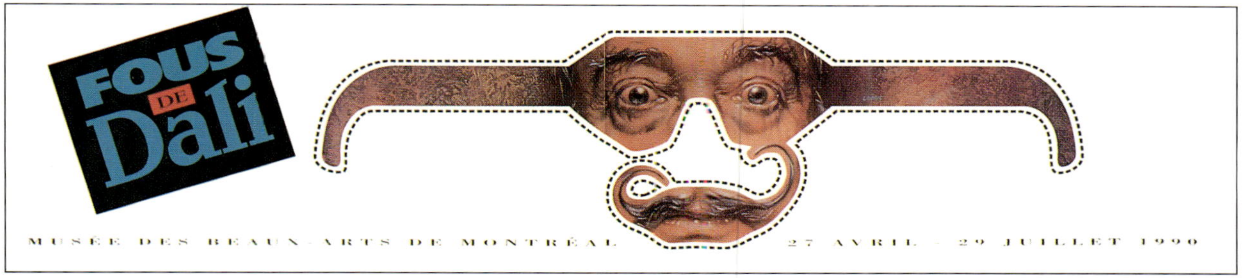

Creative Director
Pierre Audet
Art Director/Designer
Pierre Drouin
Design Agency
FOUG, Montréal
Illustrator
Bernard Leduc
Copywriter
Michel Lopez
Client
Montréal Museum of Fine Arts

Creative Director
Pierre Audet
Art Director/Designer
Pierre Drouin
Design Agency
FOUG, Montréal
Illustrator
Riopelle
Copywriter
Michel Lopez
Client
Montréal Museum of Fine Arts

Creative Director
Pierre Audet
Art Director/Designer
Pierre Drouin
Design Agency
FOUG, Montréal
Illustrator
Bernard Leduc
Photographer
André Cornellier
Copywriter
Michel Lopez
Client
Montréal Museum of Fine Arts

HEAVEN & EARTH
FINE FOOD & MORE AT THE SAINT LOUIS ART MUSEUM

HEART & SOUL
CREATIVE CLASSES & MORE AT THE SAINT LOUIS ART MUSEUM

Art Director/Designer
Margaret Coates
Design Agency
Louis London, St. Louis
Photographers
Jon Bruton & Museum Staff Photographers
Copywriters
S. Voth, S. Hunt, A. Gartland, Margaret Coates
Client
St. Louis Art Museum

DINING & DANCING
FINE FOOD & MORE AT THE SAINT LOUIS ART MUSEUM

MARILYN & MADONNA
CLASSIC FILM & MORE AT THE SAINT LOUIS ART MUSEUM

STARS & STRIPES
CLASSIC FILM & MORE AT THE SAINT LOUIS ART MUSEUM

HEAVY METAL & WRAP
UNIQUE GIFTS & MORE AT THE SAINT LOUIS ART MUSEUM

Art Director/Designer
Margaret Coates
Design Agency
Louis London, St. Louis
Photographers
Jon Bruton & Museum Staff Photographers
Copywriters
S. Voth, S. Hunt, A. Gartland, Margaret Coates
Client
St. Louis Art Museum

SEE THE EMPEROR'S CLOTHES.
IMPERIAL SILKS · MINNEAPOLIS INSTITUTE OF ARTS

Creative Director
Bill Johnson
Art Director/Designer
Christopher Cole
Design Agency
Chuck Ruhr Advertising, Minneapolis
Photographer
M.I.A.
Copywriter
Carl Pfirman
Client
Minneapolis Institute of Art

Too bad rush hour doesn't have a winner's circle.
Del Mar
July 24–Sept. 11

Art Director/Designer
Mike Hall
Design Agency
Phillips-Ramsey, San Diego
Photographer
Tom Ables
Copywriter
Cam Davis
Client
Del Mar

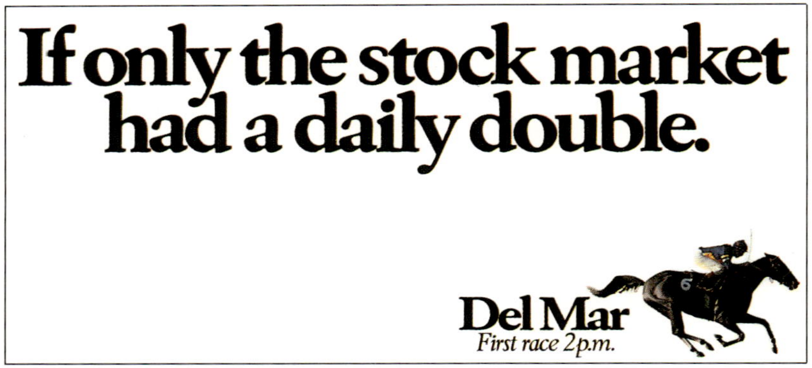
If only the stock market had a daily double.
Del Mar
First race 2p.m.

Too bad Lotto numbers don't try harder to win.
Del Mar
First race 2p.m.

High speed chase near I-5. Film at 11.
Del Mar
First race 2p.m.

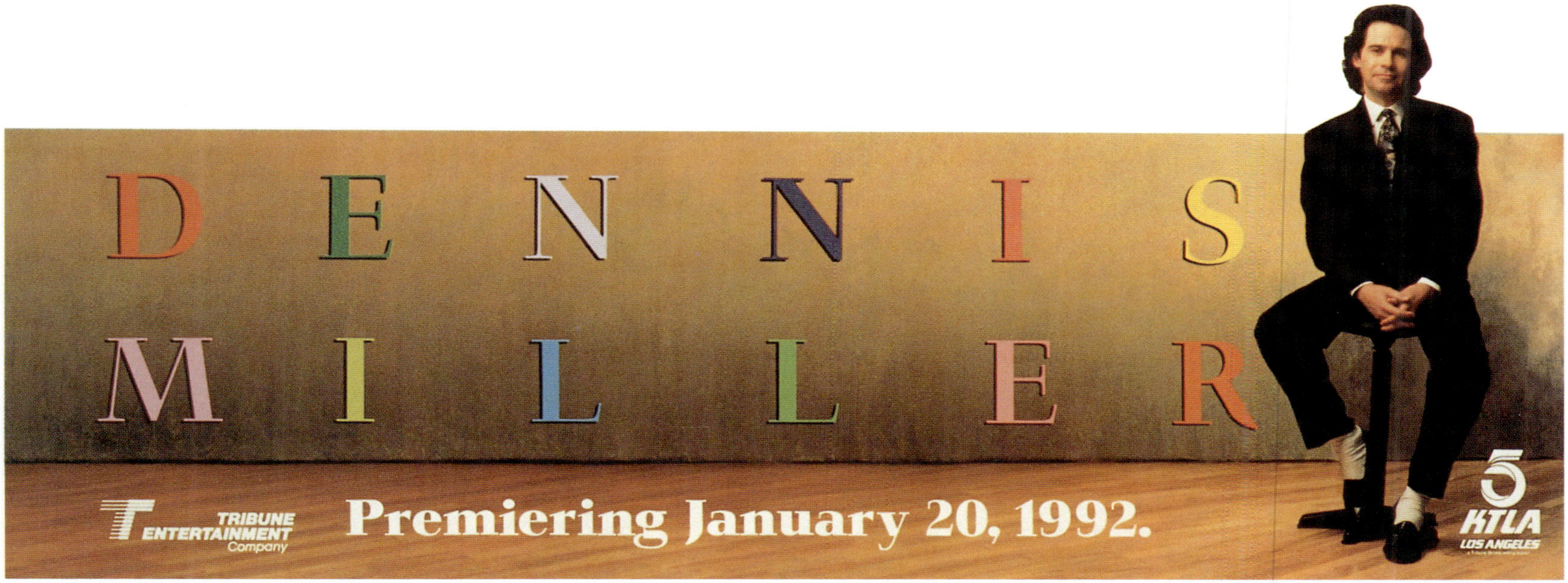

Creative Director
Mike Waterkotte
Art Director
Randy Tatum
Designer
Gabe Difiore
Design Agency
Eisaman, Johns & Laws, Chicago
Photographer
Jean Moss
Copywriter
Ron Lazzeretti
Client
Tribune Entertainment

Art Director
John Vitro
Design Agency
Franklin & Associates, San Diego
Copywriter
John Robertson
Client
San Diego Zoo

Creative Director
Bob Kwait
Designer
Bob Kwait
Design Agency
Phillips-Ramsey, San Diego
Photographer
Ron Larrison
Copywriter
Bob Kwait
Client
San Diego Zoo

Art Directors
Stephanie Benton, John Green
Designer
Stephanie Benton
Design Agency
Bauerlein Advertising, New Orleans
Photographer
Dublin Studios
Copywriter
John Green
Client
Audubon Institute

San Diego's most popular hangout.
The San Diego Zoo
GANNETT OUTDOOR

YOUR KIDS BELONG IN THE ZOO.
(Free October 1-31)
San Diego Zoo

OUTDOOR SYSTEMS
Two thumbs up.
AUDUBON ZOO

Flights
Leaving Daily
12:30 4:45
Miami
Seaquarium®
Tons of Fun
Capture The Moment On Kodak Film
Kodak Film
ACKERLEY

Art Director
Bruce Turkel
Designer
Don Cross
Design Agency
Turkel Advertising, Coconut Grove
Illustrator
Gary Carter
Copywriter
Bruce Turkel
Client
Seaquarium, Aquatic Entertainment Show/ Center

Twin Peeks.
BLANK PARK
ZOO
Des Moines Parks and Recreation
NAEGELE

Art Director/Designer
Bill McKnight
Design Agency
Universal Outdoor Advertising, Des Moines
Copywriter
Bill McKnight
Client
Blank Park Zoo

CASH, CZECH OR AMERICAN EXPRESS?
The Stella Artois. Queen's Club. June 11-17. Tickets 081-741 8999
STELLA ARTOIS

Creative Director
Adrian Holmes
Art Director
Simon Butler
Design Agency
Lowe Howard-Spink, England
Illustrator
Sebastian Krüger
Copywriter
Gethin Stout
Client
Whitbread

Creative/Art Director
Chris Hughes
Designer
Chris Hughes
Design Agency
The Chris Hughes Company, Toronto
Photographer
Frank Clarke & Associates
Copywriters
Chris Hughes, Jim Boco
Client
Second City

SACRED COWS ROASTED NIGHTLY.
the Second City.
LEGENDARY COMEDY
DINNER THEATRE • CALL 863-1111 • SHOW ONLY

Man-eating Shark.
Man, eating Shark.
Carlos Murphy's

Have you tried our spicy carrots?
Carlos Murphy's

HOT.
You know, people are a lot like salsa.
MILD.
Carlos Murphy's

1,200 fish tacos served daily.
(Good thing the Ocean's Nearby.)
Carlos Murphy's

He's not so Scary when he's wrapped in a tortilla.
Carlos Murphy's

Art Director
John Smith
Design Agency
Lambesis Communications, San Diego
Copywriter
John Jones
Client
Carlos Murphy's

Creative Director
Kan Tai-Keung
Art Directors
Kan Tai-Keung, Freeman Lau Siu Hong
Design Agency
Kan Tai-Keung Design & Associates, Hong Kong
Designer/Illustrator
Eddy Yu Chi Kong
Client
The Urban Council

The 11th Hong Kong International Film Festival
第十一屆香港國際電影節
April 10–25, 1987
一九八七年四月十日至二十五日
City Hall • Space Museum
Columbia Classics Cinema
Presented by the Urban Council

The 11th Hong Kong International Film Festival • Cantonese Opera Films Retrospective
第十一屆香港國際電影節·粵語戲曲片回顧

CHINESE
PAINTINGS
EXHIBITION
BY 13
HONG KONG
ARTISTS
OSAKA
JAPAN
香港在住 13作家による
水墨画展

Art Director/Designer
Kan Tai-Keung
Design Agency
Kan Tai-Keung Design & Associates, Hong Kong
Photographer
Wong Ching Kong
Client
Hong Kong Trade Development Council

Creative Director
Martin Jewett
Art Director/Designer
Kevin Lippy
Design Agency
Doe-Anderson
Advertising Agency,
Louisville
Copywriter
Ed Neary
Client
Courier Journal

Nothing Attracts People Like Courier-Journal Classifieds.
OUTDOOR SYSTEMS

Creative Director
David Abbott
Art Director
Ron Brown
Design Agency
Abbott Mead Vickers,
England
Copywriter
David Abbott
Client
The Economist

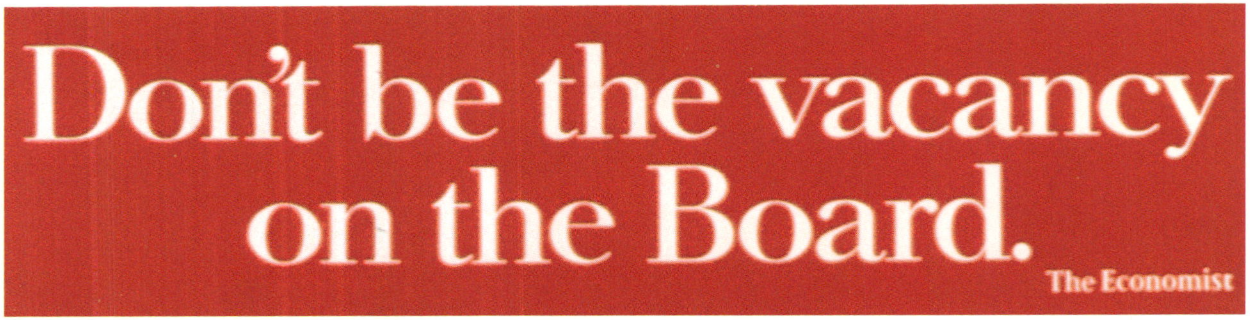
Don't be the vacancy on the Board.
The Economist

In the global village read the local paper.
The Economist

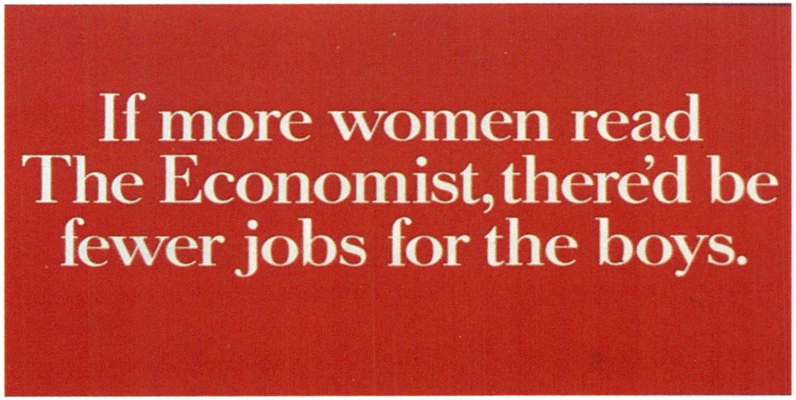
If more women read The Economist, there'd be fewer jobs for the boys.

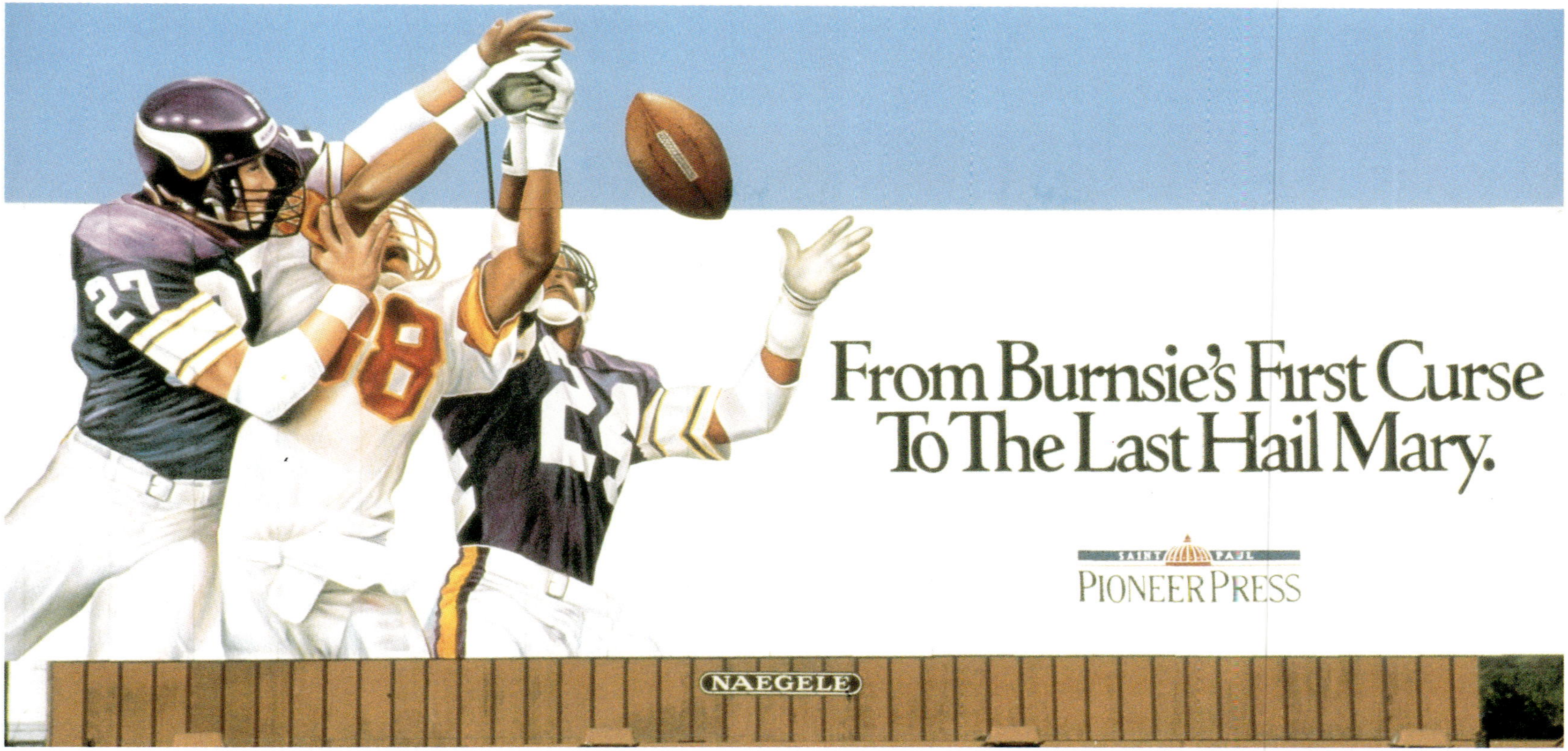
From Burnsie's First Curse
To The Last Hail Mary.
SAINT PAUL
PIONEER PRESS
NAEGELE

Creative Director
Jac Coverdale
Art Director
Craig Tanimoto
Design Agency
Clarity Coverdale Rueff, Minneapolis
Copywriter
Lee Schmidt
Client
St. Paul Pioneer Press

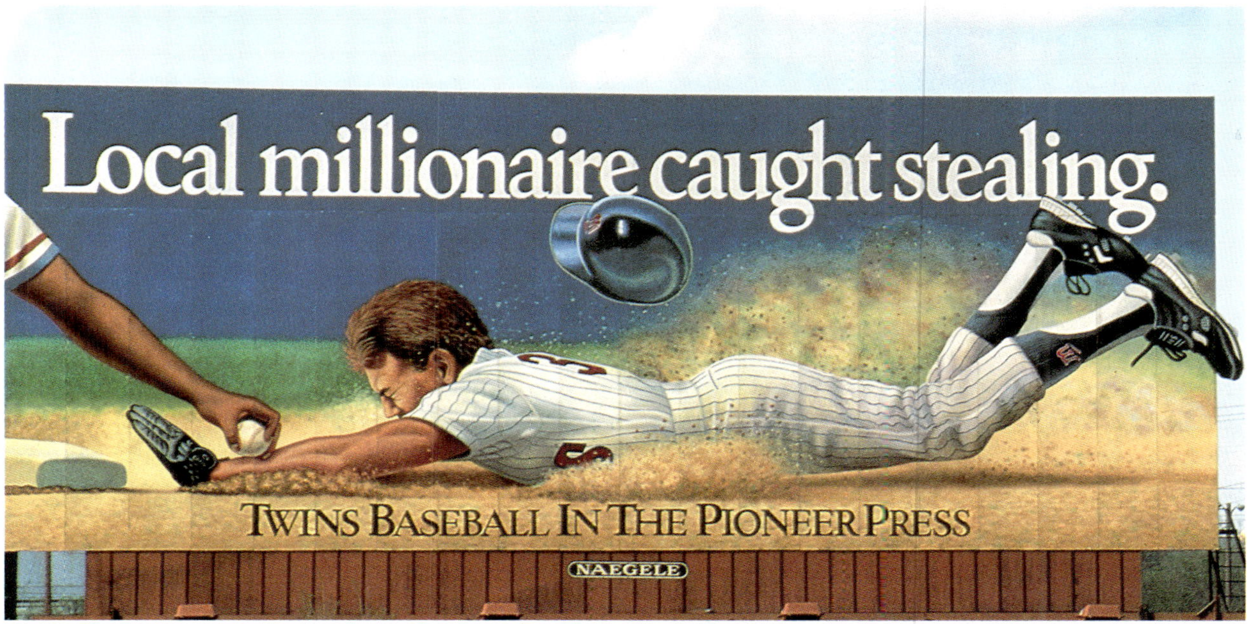
Local millionaire caught stealing.
TWINS BASEBALL IN THE PIONEER PRESS
NAEGELE

Creative Director
Jac Coverdale
Design Agency
Clarity Coverdale Rueff, Minneapolis
Illustrator
Dan Craig
Copywriter
Jerry Fury
Client
St. Paul Pioneer Press

Art Director
Jeremy Postaer
Design Agency
Goodby Berlin & Silverstein, San Francisco
Photographers
Dan Escobar, Stock photos
Copywriter
Rob Bagot
Client
San Francisco Examiner

A Lot Can Happen Between 9&5.
San Francisco Examiner
The Afternoon Paper.

A Lot Can Happen Between 9&5.
U.S. ARMY
San Francisco Examiner
The Afternoon Paper.

A Lot Can Happen Between 9&5.
Roger Craig at work, above
macy's
San Francisco Examiner
The Afternoon Paper.

A Lot Can Happen Between 9&5.
ROGER CRAIG FOR CHRISTOPHER HAYES
macy's
ROGER CRAIG FOR WILDMAN WATERWEAR.
CORKY'S SURF SHOP
San Francisco Examiner
The Afternoon Paper.

Creative Director
Pat Burnham
Art Director
Bob Brihn
Design Agency
Fallon McElligott, Minneapolis
Copywriter
Phil Hanft
Client
Star Tribune Newspaper

COMPLETE COVERAGE OF LOCAL ROCK GROUPS.
Star Tribune
NAEGELE

OUR PAPER HAS IMPORTANT NEWS
FOR BOTH HEMISPHERES.
Star Tribune
© Star Tribune 1991

Creative Director
Pat Burnham
Art Director
Bob Brihn
Design Agency
Fallon McElligott,
Minneapolis
Copywriter
Phil Hanft
Client
Star Tribune Newspaper

Creative Director
John Muller
Art Director
Scott Chapman
Designer
Mike Regner
Design Agency
Muller & Co., Kansas City
Photographer
David Marks
Copywriter
The Des Moines Register
Client
The Des Moines Register

BYE-BYE BIRDIE.
KISS IT GOODBYE IN THE REGISTER CLASSIFIEDS. 284-8141.
NAEGELE

SOLD
HAVE AN ORGAN REMOVED.
SS IT GOODBYE IN THE REGISTER CLASSIFIEDS. 284-8141.
NAEGELE

KISS THAT SUCKER GOODBYE.
CALL THE DES MOINES REGISTER CLASSIFIEDS 284-8141.
NAEGELE

NO ONE COVERS FOOD LIKE THE REGISTER.
SUBSCRIBE TODAY. 284-8311.
NAEGELE

Creative Director
John Muller
Art Director
Scott Chapman
Designer
Mike Regner
Design Agency
Muller & Co., Kansas City
Photographer
David Marks
Copywriter
The Des Moines Register
Client
The Des Moines Register

NO ONE COVERS SPORTS LIKE THE REGISTER.
SUBSCRIBE TODAY. 284-8311.
THE BIG PEACH
NAEGELE

NO ONE COVERS BUSINESS LIKE THE REGISTER.
SUBSCRIBE TODAY. 284-8311.
NAEGELE

Campbell's
SOUP
The cure for
the common cold.
MEDIACOM

Campbell's
SOUP
Puts colour
in your cheeks.
MEDIACOM

Art Director
Jim Brown
Design Agency
Ogilvy & Mather,
Toronto
Copywriter
Brad Myers
Client
Campbell Soup Co.

Campbell's
SOUP
Better than a sweater
MEDIACOM

Campbell's
SOUP
Unwind.
MEDIACOM

Creative Director
Lee Clow
Art Directors
Pam Cunningham, Dennis Mickaelian, Gail San Filippo
Design Agency
Chiat/Day/Mojo Inc., Venice
Photographer
Paul Gersten
Copywriter
Hillary Jordan
Client
Foster Farms

It never freezes
in these parts.
FOSTER FARMS
FRESH
FRYING CHICKEN
DRUMSTICKS
CALIFORNIA GROWN

Legally fresh.
Morally fresh.
Fresh Chicken
FOSTER FARMS
FRESH
FRYING CHICKEN
DRUMSTICKS
CALIFORNIA GROWN

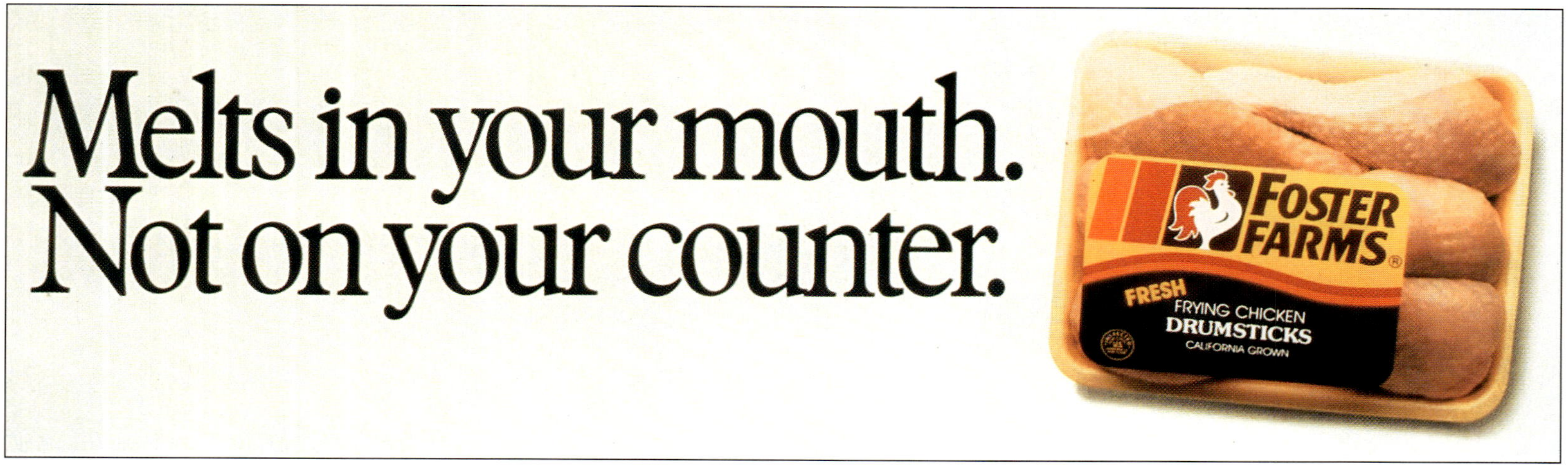
Melts in your mouth.
Not on your counter.
FOSTER FARMS
FRESH
FRYING CHICKEN
DRUMSTICKS
CALIFORNIA GROWN

Why Cops In Texas
Don't Eat Donuts.
Tippin's
RESTAURANT & PIE PANTRY

We Lay It On Thicker
Than Politicians.
Tippin's
RESTAURANT & PIE PANTRY

Now Entering The
State Of Euphoria.
Tippin's
RESTAURANT & PIE PANTRY

Creative Director
Bill Johnson
Art Director/Designer
Brien Spanier
Design Agency
Chuck Ruhr Advertising, Minneapolis
Photographers
Marvy!, Shawn Michienzi
Copywriter
Josh Denberg
Client
Tippins

Art Director
Bob Kovanda
Design Agency
J. Walter Thompson, Chicago
Copywriter
Larry Lipson

Get eggs without scrambling around town.
Better dairy selection, now at
7 ELEVEN

Groceries without the gridlock.
More groceries, less stress, now at
7 ELEVEN

Grapes without the wrath.
Fresh produce, now at
ELEVEn
At Participating Stores
The Southland Corporation

Design Agency
Cossette Communication-Marketing
Client
Supermarchés Provigo Inc.

romaine
iceberg
frisée
escarole
chicorée
Boston, P.Q.
Au Québec on retrouve une grande variété de laitues ◆ On doit déchiqueter la laitue avec les mains et éviter le couteau qui la fait rouiller ◆ Il ne faut l'assaisonner qu'au moment de servir pour préserver les vitamines et minéraux qu'elle contient ◆ Combiner plusieurs variétés de laitue est une bonne façon de relever la saveur autant que le coup d'œil.
Parce que nous savons que la fraîcheur pour vous, c'est important.
Quand on veut plus. Provigo.

Notre Pois Fait le Poids.
Comme chacun de nos petits pois, chacun des produits qui porte la marque Provigo, a été longuement choisi, mesuré, évalué et approuvé par les spécialistes de la qualité du laboratoire de Provigo ◆ Quand le nom Provigo est apposé, c'est qu'il s'agit d'un produit qui se compare hautement aux grandes marques ◆ À qualité égale, la marque Provigo a l'avantage du prix.
Parce que nous savons que vous voulez toujours ce qu'il y a de mieux pour votre argent.
Quand on veut plus. Provigo.

Notre Pain Quotidien.
La recette du pain est millénaire et pourtant la seule odeur du pain qui cuit, suffit encore à faire frémir les papilles ◆ Qu'il soit crouté, au lait, aux oeufs, en miche, en tranche, en baguette, le pain est débordant de nature et toujours frais chez Provigo ◆ Tous les jours nous cuisons baguettes et croissants pour que notre pain quotidien soit le meilleur.
Parce que nous savons que la fraîcheur fait toute la différence.
Quand on veut plus. Provigo.

Kiwis, Kakis et Cie.
Provigo cueille ses fruits partout dans le monde. Les fruits sont tous fragiles; même après la cueillette, ils continuent à vivre ◆ Il faut éviter de les laisser à la température ambiante ◆ Le jus d'agrume aide les fruits comme la pomme, la poire et la banane à éviter le brunissement ◆ Kiwis, kakis, mangues, papayes, caramboles et Cie, rien ne vaut la variété.
Parce que nous savons que la variété pour vous, c'est important.
Quand on veut plus. Provigo.

OLÉ!
LU
ET
APPROUVÉ

LES MURS ONT DES OREILLES.
LU
ET
APPROUVÉ

Art Director
Lucie Pardo
Design Agency
BELIER, France
Photographer
Gérard Beaulet
Copywriter
Vincent Pambarguian
Client
LU

ACTE MANQUÉ.
NANTES
LU
ET

PETIT CREUX.
LU

How do you stop
a pterrifying
Pterodactyl from
scaring a cavemum
and her baby?
You bite
its wings
off.
VOLCANO VALLEY
Every bite's an adventure.

How do you stop
a dragon
from breathing
fire on a
brave knight?
You bite
its nose
off.
WIZARD'S CASTLE
Every bite's an adventure.

Art Director/Designer
Brian Harrod
Design Agency
Harrod & Mirlin, Toronto
Illustrator
Roger Hill

Copywriter
Ian Mirlin
Client
Christie Brown & Co.

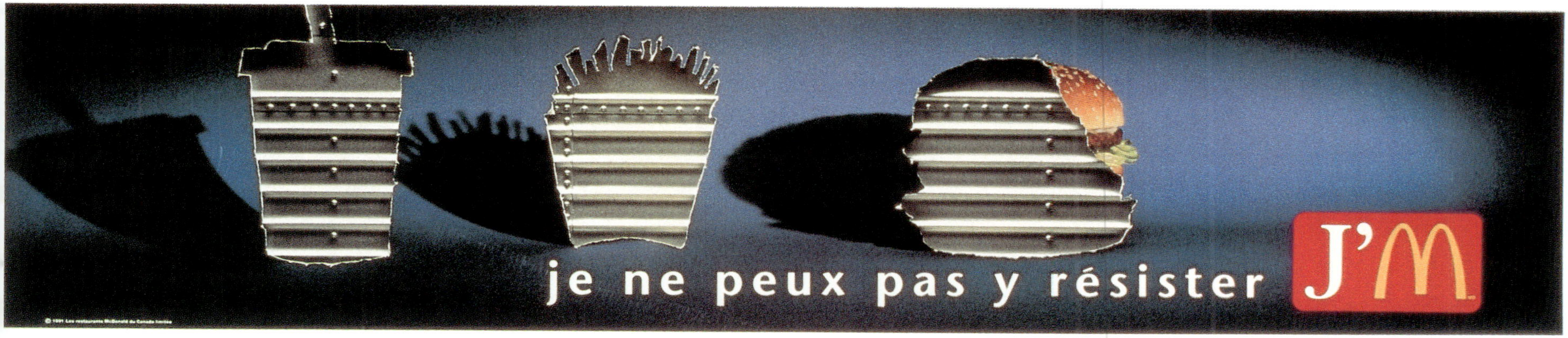
je ne peux pas y résister
J'M

Pizza!
MEDIACOM

McDonald's
je ne peux pas y résister
J'M

Design Agency
Cosstte Communication-Marketing, Montréal
Client
McDonald Restaurant of Canada

Design Agency
Cosstte Communication-Marketing, Montréal
Client
McDonald Restaurant of Canada

Creative Director
Leon Berger
Art Director
Uno Ramat
Design Agency
Young & Rubicam, Montreal
Copywriter
Cameron Miller
Client
Johnson & Johnson

Creative Director
Leon Berger
Art Director
Sue Boivin
Design Agency
Young & Rubicam, Montreal
Copywriter
Martin-Eric Ouellette
Client
Johnson & Johnson

WE'RE STUCK ON KIDS.
NEW FROM BAND-AID

STUCK MAY 29
AND STILL HOLDING
TRY BAND-AID FABRIC
HOOK

Bad breath can upset your morning.
Fortunately, fresh breath is a spray away.
Binaca

Art Director/Designer
Jeff Layton
Design Agency
Jeff Layton & Assoc. Ltd./Grey Canada, Toronto
Illustrator/Photographer
Terry Puplett, Sharpshooter Studios
Copywriter
Jim Catlin
Client
Airwick Canada

Creative Director
Tim Delaney
Art Director
Steve Dunn
Design Agency
Leagas Delaney, England
Photographer
Peter Lindberg
Copywriter
Tim Delaney
Client
Revlon

WHEN THE EARTH MOVES, YOUR LIPSTICK SHOULDN'T FOLLOW IT.
REVLON
Colour Memory. The lipstick that keeps its colour.

C'est beau, mais c'est quoi?
Bien pensé
IKEA

C'est beau, mais c'est quoi?
Bien pensé
IKEA

Creative Director
Pierre Audet
Art Director/Designer
Pierre Drouin
Design Agency
FOUG, Montréal
Photographer
André Cornellier
Copywriter
Michel Lopez
Client
IKEA

C'est beau, mais c'est quoi?
Bien pensé
IKEA

Windshield Wiper.
Sunlight
The New All-Purpose Sunlight Cloth
Sunlight

Rub-a-tub-tub.
Sunlight
The New All-Purpose Sunlight Cloth
Sunlight

Creative Director
Bill Durnan
Art Director
Benjamin BenSimon
Design Agency
MacLaren:Lintas, Toronto
Photographer
Shin Sugion
Copywriter
David Innis
Client
Lever Brothers (Sunlight)

Seabrook. That About Covers It.
NAEGELE
Memphis, Tn.

Creative Director
Michael H. Thompson
Art Director/Designer
Trace Hallowell
Design Agency
Thompson & Company, Memphis
Copywriters
Michael H. Thompson, Mickey Hodges
Client
Seabrook Wallcoverings

(Should've Gone To Seabrook)
NAEGELE
Memphis, Tn.

HUNDREDS OF GUITARS TO PICK FROM.
Guitar Center
2059 N. Snelling, Roseville MN 631-9424

Our Best Deals Have Strings Attached.
Guitar Center
2059 N. Snelling, Roseville MN 631-9424

Buy A Guitar Without A Fret.
Guitar Center
2059 N. Snelling, Roseville MN 631-9424

Creative Director
Bert Gardner
Art Director/Designer
Steve Mitchell
Design Agency
Bozell Inc., Minneapolis
Copywriter
Doug Adkins
Client
Guitar Center

IBM

IBM

IBM

Creative Directors
Ron Meijer, Henry van Varik
Art Directors
Henry van Varik, Enrico Bartens
Design Agency
GGK, Amsterdam
Photographers
Leen Thijsse, Chris Lewis
Copywriters
Ron Meijer, Machteld van der Gaag
Client
IBM

Art Director/Designer
Clodagh Wheatley
Design Agency
Wheatley & Rosenberg, Montréal
Photographer
Michel Pilon
Client
Chausseurs ALDO Shoes

Creative Director
Ken Hoggins
Art Directors
Jamie Way, David Christensen
Design Agency
Lowe Howard-Spink, England
Photographer
Peter Lavery
Client
Reebok

Think of them as hush puppies in heat.
THIEVES MARKET
THROUGHOUT SOUTHERN CALIFORNIA
Justin
GANNETT OUTDOOR

No lady should live in a shoe.
THIEVES MARKET
Zodiac
GANNETT OUTDOOR

We wouldn't want to be in your shoes.
THIEVES MARKET
Tony Lama
BOOTS
GANNETT OUTDOOR

There are millions of square feet in L.A.
THIEVES MARKET
Justin
On Beverly at La Cienega.
GANNETT OUTDOOR

Creative Director
Cary Sacks
Art Director/Designer
David Duncan
Design Agency
Sacks/Fuller Advertising, Los Angeles
Illustrator
David Duncan
Copywriter
Cary Sacks
Client
Thieves Market

Art Director
Oliviero Toscani
Design Agency
Benetton Services Corp., Italy

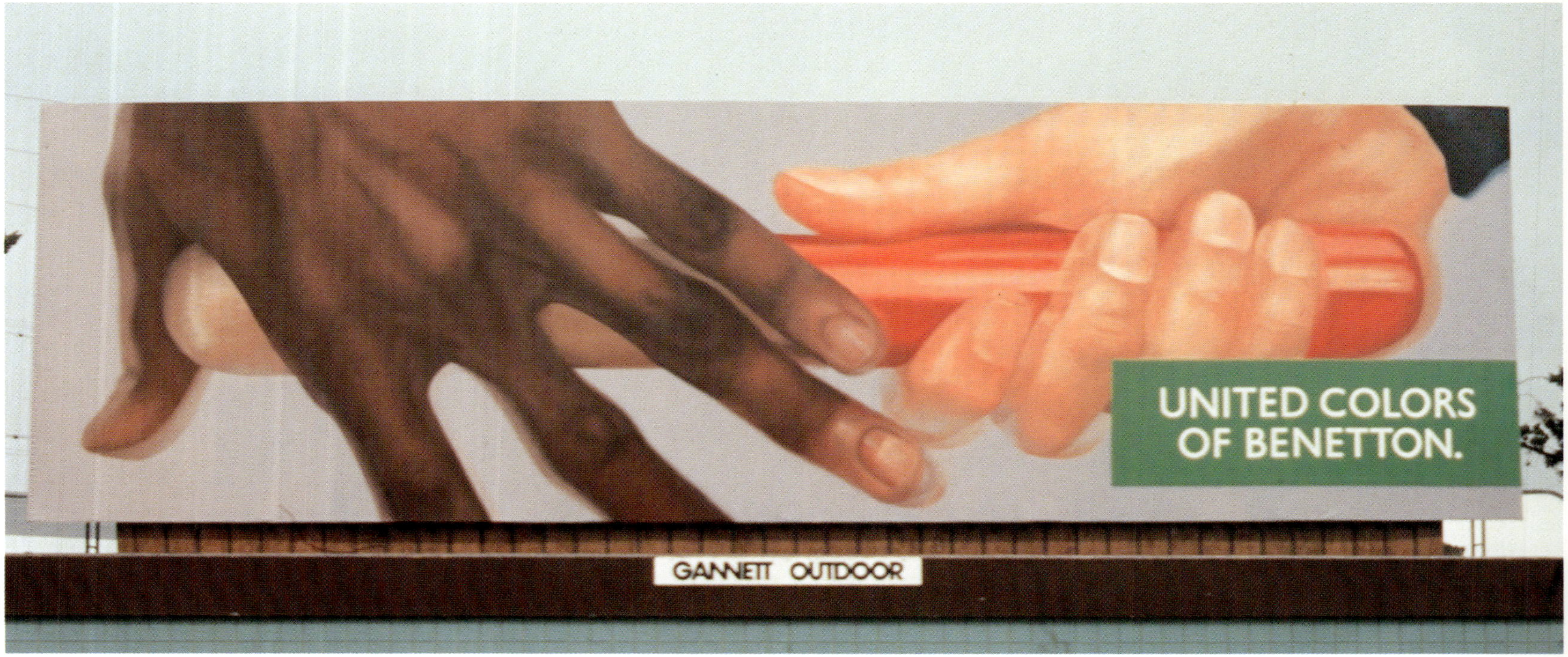

UNITED COLORS
OF BENETTON.
GANNETT OUTDOOR

UNITED COLORS
OF BENETTON.

Creative Director/ Designer
Brian Harrod
Design Agency
Harrod & Mirlin, Toronto
Photographer
Bert Bell
Copywriter
Grahame Arnould
Client
Levi Strauss & Co.

Art Director/Designer
Dianne Eastman
Design Agency
Harrod & Mirlin, Toronto
Photographer
Bert Bell
Copywriter
Bill Daniel
Client
Levi Strauss & Co

Comfort
and joy.
Levi's

Recycle.
Levi's

...and a partridge in a pair tree
Levi's
MEDIACOM

Levi Strauss & Co.
Levi's
Merry Christmas and a Happy New Pair.
MEDIACOM

Art Director/Designer
James Jung
Design Agency
Harrod & Mirlin, Toronto
Illustrator
Desmond Montague
Copywriter
Grahame Arnould
Client
Levi Strauss & Co.

Art Director/Designer
Mel McKelvie
Design Agency
Harrod & Mirlin, Toronto
Illustrator
Desmond Montague
Copywriter
Grahame Arnould
Client
Levi Strauss & Co.

Art Director/Designer
James Jung
Design Agency
Harrod & Mirlin, Toronto
Photographer
Tim Saunders
Copywriter
Brent Peterson
Client
Levi Strauss & Co.

Art Director/Designer
James Jung
Design Agency
Harrod & Mirlin, Toronto
Photographer
Vince Noguchi
Copywriter
Charles Dickens
Client
Levi Strauss & Co.

Knöw well.
Levi's

Christmas past.
Christmas present.
Levi's

Levi's
Split ends.

Art Directors/Designers
Brian Harrod, Dianne Eastman
Design Agency
Harrod & Mirlin, Toronto
Photographer
Shin Sugino
Copywriter
Ashley O'Brien
Client
Levi Strauss & Co.

Art Director/Designer
James Jung
Design Agency
Harrod & Mirlin, Toronto
Photographer
Vince Noguchi
Copywriter
Ian Mirlin
Client
Levi Strauss & Co.

Be cool. It's strange out there.
Levi's

Art Director/Designer
Dianne Eastman
Design Agency
Harrod & Mirlin, Toronto
Photographer
Bert Bell
Copywriters
Bill Daniel, Tony Spencer
Client
Levi Strauss & Co.

Art Director/Designer
James Jung
Design Agency
Harrod & Mirlin, Toronto
Photographer
Bert Bell
Copywriters
Bill Daniel, Grahame Arnould
Client
Levi Strauss & Co.

Always travel in pairs.
LEVI STRAUSS & CO.
LEVI'S

Life without Levi's.

A friend to the end.
Levi's

The stories they could tell.
Levi's

Art Director/Designer
Dianne Eastman
Design Agency
Harrod & Mirlin, Toronto
Photographer
Bert Bell
Copywriter
Grahame Arnould
Client
Levi Strauss & Co.

Some assembly required.
Levi's
501

Art Director/Designer
James Jung
Design Agency
Harrod & Mirlin, Toronto
Photographer
Bert Bell
Copywriter
Bob Goulart
Client
Levi Strauss & Co.

Art Director/Designer
James Jung
Design Agency
Harrod & Mirlin, Toronto
Photographer
Bert Bell
Copywriter
Bill Daniel
Client
Levi Strauss & Co.

Lord of the flies.
Levi's
501

Sit on it.
Levi's

Fly this way. Levi's 501.

Art Director/Designer
James Jung
Design Agency
Harrod & Mirlin, Toronto
Illustrator
Dan Fell
Copywriter
Ian Mirlin
Client
Levi Strauss & Co.

Art Director/Designer
James Jung
Design Agency
Harrod & Mirlin, Toronto
Illustrator
Jacobson Fernandez
Copywriter
Ian Mirlin
Client
Levi Strauss & Co.

Art Director/Designer
Dianne Eastman
Design Agency
Harrod & Mirlin, Toronto
Photographer
Tim Saunders
Copywriter
Dianne Eastman
Client
Great Western Garment Co.

SPORTS
GREAT WESTERN GARMENT COMPANY
RILEY PANTS

Art Director
Rene Lesko
Design Agency
Paul Marciano
Advertising, Los Angeles

COLLECTION
PULSATING SENSATION FROM 兀
的·躍·動

MENSWEAR
PULSATING SENSATION FROM 兀
的·躍·動

FROM HERE,
IT LOOKS LIKE
YOU COULD USE SOME
NEW UNDERWEAR
BAMBOO LINGERIE

Art Director
Kan Tai-Keung
Designer
Eddy Yu Chi Kong
Design Agency
Kan Tai-Keung Design & Assoc. Ltd., Hong Kong
Photographer
Leung Ka Tai
Client
Copperfield Company

Art Director
Risa Mickenberg
Design Agency
Kirshenbaum & Bond, New York
Copywriter
Risa Mickenberg
Client
Bamboo Lingerie

Art Director/Designer
Dianne Eastman
Design Firm/Agency
Harrod & Mirlin, Toronto
Photographer
Bert Bell /Stock Photo
Copywriter
Ian Mirlin
Client
Evian Source de France

Art Director
Grahame Arnould
Design Agency
Harrod & Mirlin, Toronto
Illustrator
Grahame Arnould
Client
Evian Source de France

FRESHLY-SQUEEZED FRENCH ALPS.
evian
evian
natural spring water

evian
MEDIACOM
GMC

PRESENTING THE NATURAL TALENT OF THE FRENCH ALPS.
evian
evian
natural spring water

CANADA DRY
New
CANADA DRY
It was a tight squeeze, but we did it.

Art Director
Doug Robinson
Design Agency
Young & Rubicam, Toronto
Copywriter
Steve Conover
Client
Canada Dry

CANADA DRY
New
CANADA DRY
'Tis the squeezin'

Creative Director
Rick Davis
Art Director/Designer
Doug Robinson
Design Agency
Young & Rubicam, Toronto
Photographer
Ian Campbell
Copywriter
Steve Conover
Client
Canada Dry

PEPSI
Gas
Guzzler
Veryfine
100% apple juice
951

Veryfine
100% apple juice
Just Drink It.
Veryfine

Revere
Gas
PEPSI
Veryfine
100% apple juice
Guzzler
7331

Veryfine
100% apple juice
Prevent
Overheating
123

Revere
Traffic Should Flow
This Smoothly.
Veryfine
fruit punch
Veryfine

Creative Director
Edward Boches
Art Directors
Brian Fandetti, Margaret McGovern
Design Agency
Mullen Advertising, Philadelphia
Photographer
Bill DeBold
Copywriters
Edward Boches, Bob Horgan
Client
Very Fine (Juice)

Creative Director
Robin Raj
Art Director
Florence Buchanan
Design Agency
Weiss, Whitten, Carroll, Stagliano, New York
Photographer
Michael Mazzeo/
Bettmann Archive-stock
Copywriters
Paul Hartzell, Robin Raj
Client
Guinness Import Company

WHAT IS MAN'S DEEPEST DESIRE?
D.H. Lawrence, 1915.
BASS HELPS YOU GET TO THE BOTTOM OF IT ALL.
BASS & Co PALE ALE
Bass

WHY DOES MAN EXIST?
Friedrich Wilhelm Nietzsche, 1882.
BASS HELPS YOU GET TO THE BOTTOM OF IT ALL.
BASS & Co PALE ALE
Bass

WHAT CAN COMPARE WITH LIFE'S SIMPLE PLEASURES?
Samuel Langhorne Clemens (Mark Twain), 1905.
BASS HELPS YOU GET TO THE BOTTOM OF IT ALL.
BASS & Co PALE ALE
Bass

CANADIAN WILDLIFE–No. 3
The Great Bellowing Moose.
Molson Canadian. What Beer's All About.

Can Say It, But Won't.
"Vee·ba·rova"
For centuries it's been the way to order Poland's finest vodka.
If You Can't Say It, You Can't Have It.

CANADIAN WILDLIFE–No. 6
The Slick-Backed Howling Wolf.
Molson Canadian. What Beer's All About.

Creative Directors
Bill Durnan, Stephen Creet, Michael McLaughlin
Art Director
Michael McLaughlin
Design Agency
MacLaren:Lintas, Toronto
Photographer
Nigel Dickson
Copywriter
Stephen Creet
Client
Molson Breweries of Canada-Molson Canadian Beer

Creative Directors
Jack Mariucci, Bob Mackall, Jane Talcott
Art Director/Designer
David Rauch
Design Agency
DDB Needham Worldwide, New York
Photographer
Lee Crum
Copywriter
Lori McNulty
Client
House of Seagram/ Wyborowa Vodka

Creative Directors
Bill Durnan, Michael McLaughlin, Stephen Creet
Art Director
Michael McLaughlin
Design Agency
MacLaren:Lintas, Toronto
Photographer
Nigel Dickson
Copywriter
Stephen Creet
Client
Molson Breweries of Canada-Molson Canadian Beer

Creative/Art Director
Ron Davidson
Design Agency
Colenso
Communications Ltd.,
New Zealand
Copywriter
Simon Moore
Client
Dominion Breweries

SWAN LIGHT WON'T
MAKE YOUR DINGO LIMP.
THE AUSTRALIAN PINT THAT'S LOW IN ALCOHOL

Creative Director
Paul Arden
Art Director
Russell Ra Ey
Design Agency
Saatchi & Saatchi, England
Copywriter
John O'Keeffe
Client
Allied Breweries

Yo ho ho and a ...
Captain Morgan
ORIGINAL
SPICED RUM
Puerto Rican Rum with Spice and Other Natural Flavors
ORIGINAL SPICED RUM
Captain Morgan
ONE LITER

Creative Directors
Jack Mariucci, Bob Mackall, Charlie Piccirillo
Art Director
Steve Jaeger
Designer
Steve Jaeger
Design Agency
DDB Needham Worldwide, New York
Photographer
Craig Cutler
Copywriter
Steve Jaeger
Client
House of Seagram/ Captain Morgan Spiced Rum

Disturb a laid-back Californian.
CALIFORNIA COOLER
CITRUS
ORANGE
PEACH
TROPICAL
California.The Drink.

Creative Director/ Designer
Brian Harrod
Design Agency
Harrod & Mirlin, Toronto
Illustrator
Roger Hill
Copywriter
Ian Mirlin
Client
Santa Fe

Art Director/Designer
James Jung
Design Agency
Harrod & Mirlin, Toronto
Illustrator
Doug Fraser
Copywriter
Bill Daniel
Client
Moosehead Breweries

TEN-PENNY ALE. THE TASTE OF INDEPENDENCE.

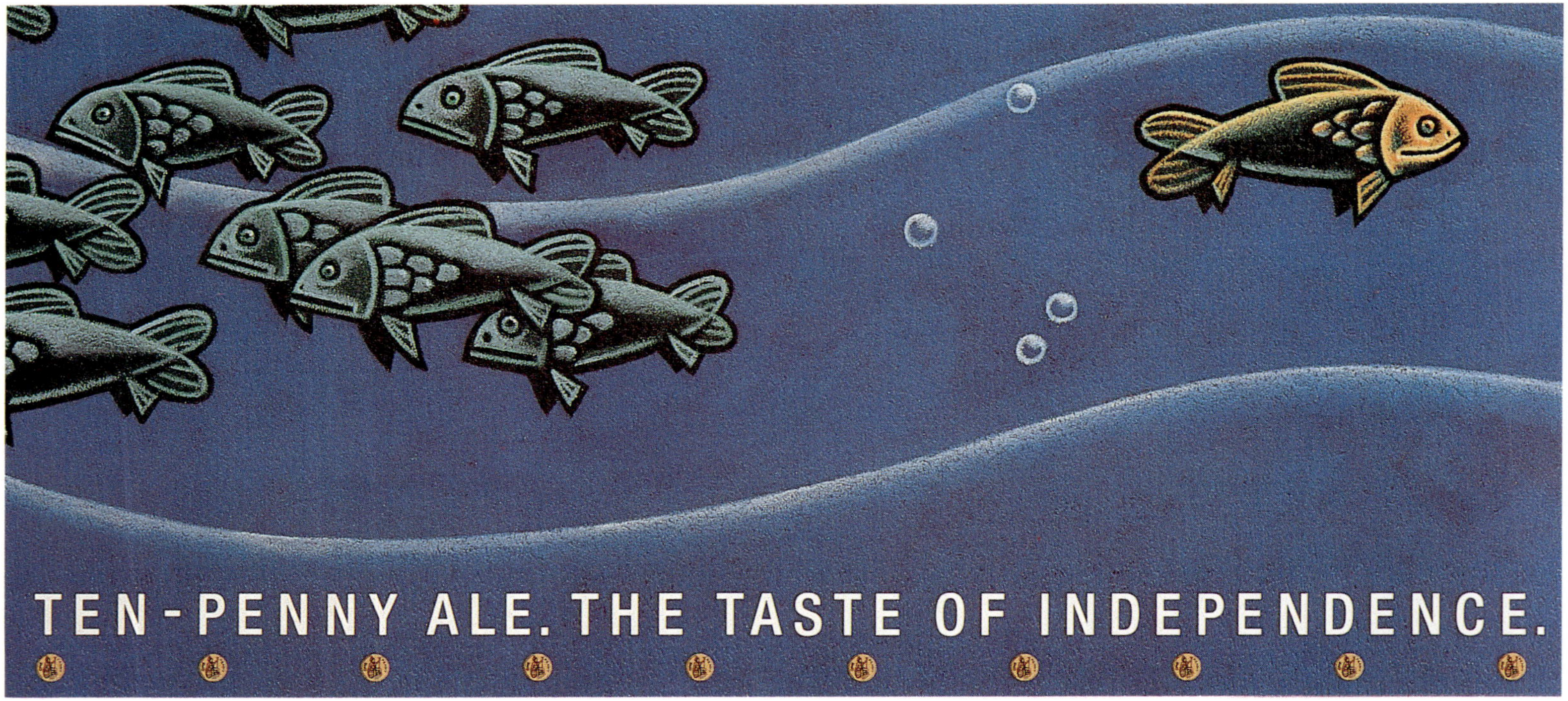
TEN-PENNY ALE. THE TASTE OF INDEPENDENCE.

It has a great future ahead of it, because it has a great story behind it.
PREMIUM
MOOSEHEAD
DRY
5.5% alc./vol.
The future of dry beer.

Because it has a great story behind it, it has a great future ahead of it.
PREMIUM DRY
MOOSEHEAD
Regular Price.
The future of dry beer.

Art Director/Designer
James Jung
Design Agency
Harrod & Mirlin, Toronto
Photographer
Tim Saunders
Copywriter
Ian Mirlin
Client
Moosehead Breweries

Art Director/Designer
James Jung
Design Agency
Harrod & Mirlin, Toronto
Photographer
Vince Noguchi
Copywriter
Ian Mirlin
Client
Moosehead Breweries

HELP FIGHT THE SPREAD OF BORING BEERS.
TEN-PENNY
Old Stock Ale
TEN-PENNY. THE TASTE OF INDEPENDENCE.

Home opener.
Alpine Light
Alpine Light

Go for the cold.
ALPINE
GENUINE
COLD FILTERED

Art Director/Designer
James Jung
Design Agency
Harrod & Mirlin, Toronto
Photographer
Vince Noguchi
Copywriter
Bill Daniel
Client
Moosehead Breweries

Art Director/Designer
James Jung
Design Agency
Harrod & Mirlin, Toronto
Photographer
Chris Freeland
Copywriter
Bill Daniel
Client
Moosehead Breweries

Art Director/Designer
James Jung
Design Agency
Harrod & Mirlin, Toronto
Photographer
Vince Noguchi
Copywriter
Bill Daniel
Client
Moosehead Breweries

Art Director
Ross Sutherland
Designer
Margaret Cusack
Design Agency
Margaret Cusack,
Brooklyn
Photographer
Margaret Cusack
Client
Maxwell House

NABOB
COFFEE
NABOB ALWAYS BRINGS THEM BACK.

Art Director/Designer
Brent Peterson
Design Agency
Harrod & Mirlin, Toronto
Photographer
Michael Rafelson
Copywriter
Brent Peterson
Client
Nabob

Design Agency
Cossette
Communication-
Marketing, Montréal
Client
Air Canada

Rapidair. Non-stop service.
Air Canada
MEDIACOM

AIR CANADA

Design Agency
Cossette
Communication-
Marketing, Montréal
Client
Air Canada

True comfort.
Executive Class™
AirCanada

Europe
10 vacation
destinations
AirCanada

Art Director
Duncan Milner
Design Agency
Chiat/Day/Mojo, Toronto
Illustrator
Jamie Bennett
Copywriter
Jack Neary
Client
Canadian Airlines
International Ltd.

MEANWHILE, OUT ON THE STREET, THE TORTURE CONTINUES...
AREN'T YOU GLAD YOU RIDE METRO.
metro

Art Director/Designer
Rich Park
Design Agency
Goldberg, Marchesano, Kohlman, Inc., Washington
Illustrator
John Thompson, Hellman Associates
Copywriters
Rich Park, Ed Stern
Client
Washington Metropolitan Area Transit Authority

MEANWHILE, OUT ON THE STREET, THE TORTURE CONTINUES...
AREN'T YOU GLAD YOU RIDE METRO.
metro

MEANWHILE, ON THE STREETS ABOVE, THE TORTURE CONTINUES...
AREN'T YOU GLAD YOU RIDE METRO.
metro

The Better Way
METROPASS
9250
RIDE OUT THE RECESSION
IN ANY ECONOMY THERE'S NO BETTER VALUE THAN METROPASS
THE BETTER WAY

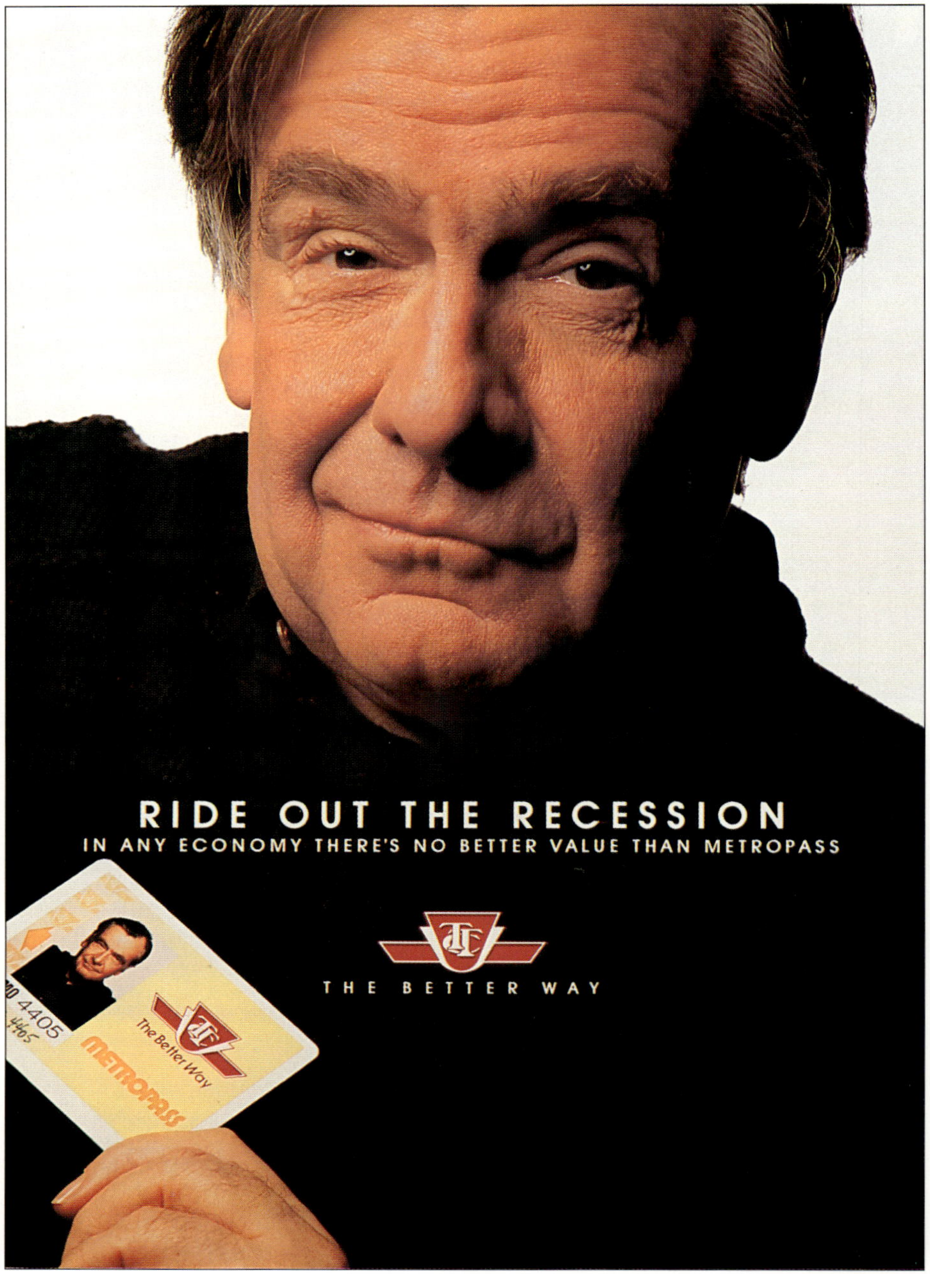
RIDE OUT THE RECESSION
IN ANY ECONOMY THERE'S NO BETTER VALUE THAN METROPASS
THE BETTER WAY
4405
The Better Way
METROPASS

RIDE OUT THE RECESSION
IN ANY ECONOMY THERE'S NO BETTER VALUE THAN METROPASS
THE BETTER WAY
The Better Way
METROPASS

RIDE OUT THE RECESSION
IN ANY ECONOMY THERE'S NO BETTER VALUE THAN METROPASS
THE BETTER WAY
The Better Way
METROPASS

Art Director
Wally Krysciak
Design Agency
McKim Advertising, Toronto
Photographer
Stephen Yeates
Copywriter
Rob Tait
Client
Toronto Transit Commission

WANT TO LEAVE THE RECESSION BEHIND?
GET ON WITH IT.
METROPASS
THE BETTER WAY

WANT TO LEAVE THE RECESSION BEHIND?
GET ON WITH IT.
METROPASS
THE BETTER WAY

WANT TO SAVE MONEY?
GET ON WITH IT.
METROPASS
THE BETTER WAY

WANT TO SAVE MONEY?
GET ON WITH IT.
METROPASS
THE BETTER WAY

Art Director
Wally Krysciak
Design Agency
McKim Advertising,
Toronto
Photographer
Stephen Yeates
Copywriter
Rob Tait
Client
Toronto Transit
Commission

SEPTEMBER
METROPASS.
WHEELS
AND
DEALS.
Your September Metropass has loads of great deals just for you:
· Varsity Blues Football
Get two adult admissions for the price of one to Blues' home games at Varsity Stadium.
· His Majesty's Feast
Save $10.00 on dinner and show any Tuesday through Friday.
· Scott's Kentucky Fried Chicken
Free 12 oz. soft drink with the purchase of any Chicken Sandwich Dinner or one free 500 ml salad with the purchase of two 500 ml salads.
· TTC Official Products
50% off selected merchandise at the Customer Centre above Davisville subway station.
For full details on these offers and over 30 more at attractions, restaurants, the theatre and tours, pick up a copy of "Customer News" on buses and streetcars. Or call the TTC Customer Centre at 393-6600.
THE BETTER WAY

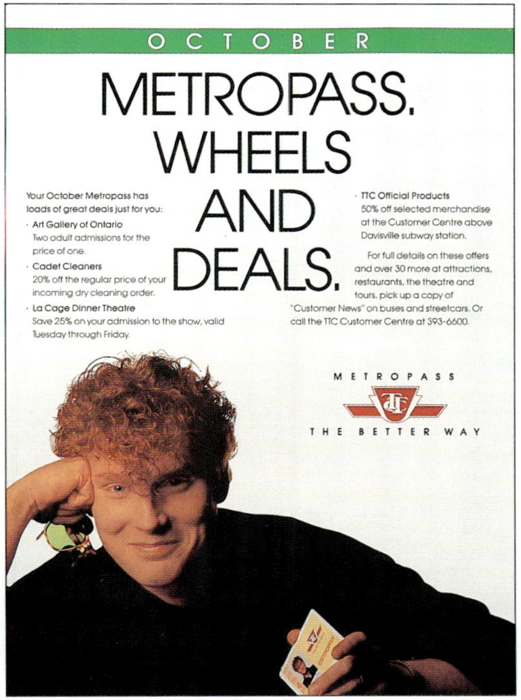
OCTOBER
METROPASS.
WHEELS
AND
DEALS.
Your October Metropass has loads of great deals just for you:
· Art Gallery of Ontario
Two adult admissions for the price of one.
· Cadet Cleaners
20% off the regular price of your incoming dry cleaning order.
· La Cage Dinner Theatre
Save 25% on your admission to the show, valid Tuesday through Friday.
· TTC Official Products
50% off selected merchandise at the Customer Centre above Davisville subway station.
For full details on these offers and over 30 more at attractions, restaurants, the theatre and tours, pick up a copy of "Customer News" on buses and streetcars. Or call the TTC Customer Centre at 393-6600.
METROPASS
THE BETTER WAY

DECEMBER
METROPASS.
WHEELS
AND
DEALS.
Your December Metropass has loads of great deals just for you:
· Music World
20% off regularly priced records, tapes, CD's and other great merchandise.
· Sparkles, CN Tower
50% off the admission Sunday to Thursday. Dine and dance overlooking the dazzling sights of Toronto from Sparkles' perch atop the CN Tower.
· Tortilla Flats
20% off regularly priced food. Enjoy the flavour of Mexico and take advantage of one delicious deal!
· TTC Official Products
50% off selected merchandise at the Customer Centre above Davisville subway station.
For full details on these offers and over 50 more at attractions, restaurants, the theatre and tours, pick up a copy of "Customer News" on buses and streetcars. Or call the TTC Customer Centre at 393-6600.
METROPASS
THE BETTER WAY

Art Director
Wally Krysciak
Design Agency
McKim Advertising, Toronto
Photographer
Stephen Yeates
Copywriter
Rob Tait
Client
Toronto Transit Commission

JANUARY
METROPASS.
WHEELS
AND
DEALS.
Your January Metropass has loads of great deals just for you:
· Music World
20% off regularly priced records, tapes, CD's and other great merchandise.
· Queen's Quay Terminal
Win one of two $500 shopping sprees! To enter just show your valid January Metropass when you visit any shop or restaurant in the Queen's Quay Terminal.
· TTC Official Products
50% off selected merchandise at the Customer Centre above Davisville subway station.
For full details on these offers and over 50 more at attractions, restaurants, the theatre and tours, pick up a copy of "Customer News" on buses, streetcars and subways. Or call the TTC Customer Centre at 393-5600. Also, look for our new Metropass Wheels and Deals Coupon book coming soon.
METROPASS
THE BETTER WAY

Art Director/Designer
John Sayles
Design Agency
Sayles Graphic Design,
Des Moines
Copywriter
Pat Turpin

THE WORLD'S FIRST SCRATCH AND SNIFF POSTER.
1 Scratch your head. 2 Sniff the air. 3 Ask yourself why you haven't moved to Milton Keynes yet.

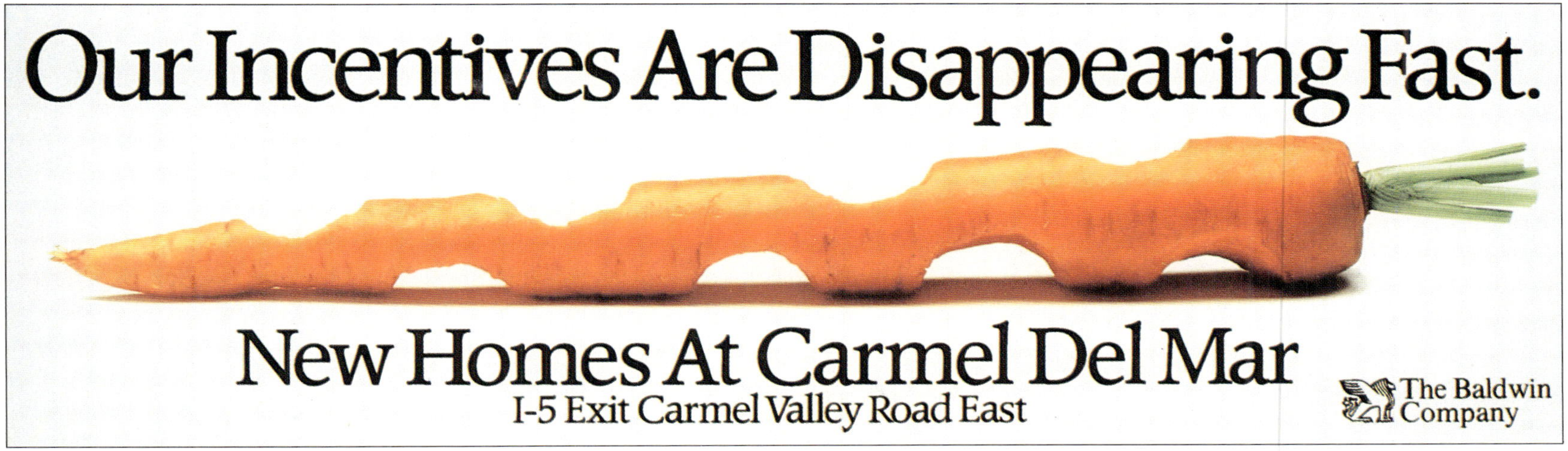
Our Incentives Are Disappearing Fast.
New Homes At Carmel Del Mar
I-5 Exit Carmel Valley Road East
The Baldwin Company

Aviara.
A Rare Resort Community.
La Costa Avenue To El Camino Real

Creative Director
Neil Anderson
Art Director
Chris Hodgkins
Design Agency
Cogent, England
Copywriter
Pip Bishop
Client
Milton Keynes Development Corp.

Art Director/Designer
Bridgit Cody
Design Agency
Phillips-Ramsey, San Diego
Copywriter
Andrea May
Client
Carmel Del Mar

Art Director/Designer
Bridgit Cody
Design Agency
Phillips-Ramsey, San Diego
Copywriter
Andrea May
Client
Aviara

Art Director
John Muller
Design Agency
Muller & Co., Kansas City
Copywriter
David Marke
Client
Summerson Burrows

SOLD
Summerson Burrows
The Fine Art of Real Estate. Summerson Burrows.

Art Director/Designer
Jim Taliana
Design Agency
DMB&B, Michigan
Photographer
McNamara Studio
Copywriter
Jim MacBeth
Client
Cadillac Motor Car Division

Cecil B. DeVille

Art Director
Todd Zwirkoski
Designer
Michael Besch
Design Agency
DMB&B, Michigan
Photographers
Chuck Gillies, Larry Dodge
Copywriter
Fred Hudler
Client
Pontiac Division/General Motors

OWN A VAN. GO.
PONTIAC
TRANS SPORT

Art Director
Tom Lichtenheld
Design Agency
Fallon McElligott, Minneapolis
Copywriter
Phil Hanft
Client
AMOCO

Any dipstick can use this oil.
Amoco
LDO
patrick

Art Director/Designer
John Sayles
Design Agency
Sayles Graphic Design, Des Moines
Client
Karl Chevrolet

Art Directors
Kerry Hilton, Kevin Moore
Design Agency
Black Gillock & Langberg, Houston
Copywriters
Kerry Hilton, Jack Fliszar, Mike Meyers
Client
Hi/Lo Auto Supply

Wingtips can fly.

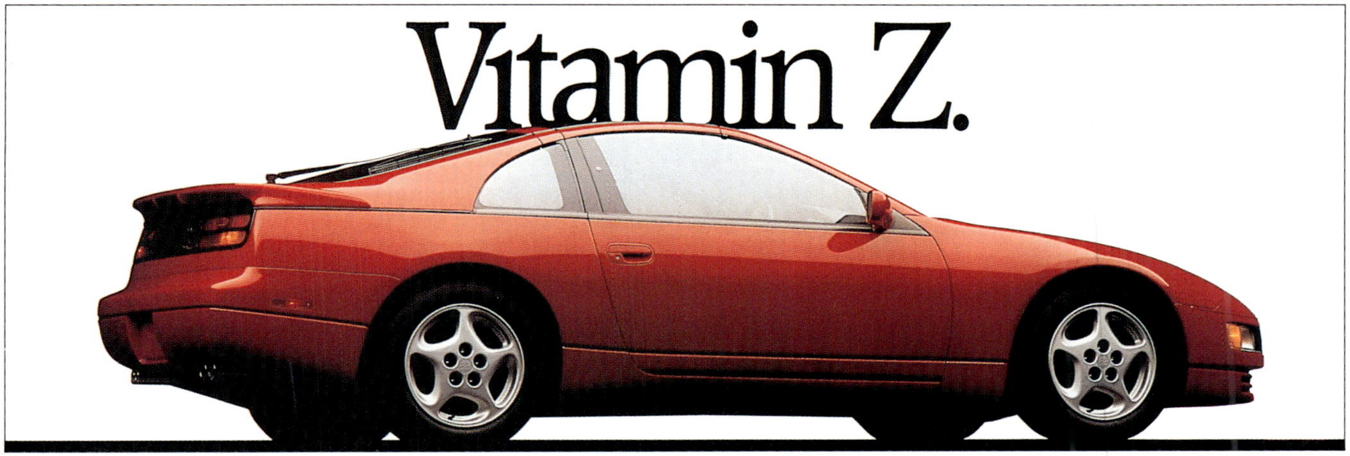
Vitamin Z.

Me Tarzan.

Art Director
Duncan Milner
Design Agency
Chiat/Day/Mojo, Toronto
Copywriter
Jack Neary
Client
Nissan Canada Inc.

Creative Director
Michael H. Thompson
Art Director/Designer
Trace Hallowell
Design Agency
Thompson & Company, Memphis
Copywriters
Trace Hallowell, Mickey Hodges
Client
United Southern Bank

Bill-Bored?
Consolidation Loans At United Southern Bank

Add On To Your Hous
e.
Home Improvement Loans At United Southern Bank

Art Director
Gerard Randall
Designer
Neil Garrison
Design Agency
Williams Company, Terre Haute
Photographer
Keith Jones
Copywriter
Gerald Randall
Client
First Federal Bank

Creative Director
Raj Marwah
Art Director
Carl Van Wijk
Design Agency
D'Arcy Masius Benton & Bowles, New Zealand
Copywriter
Raj Marwah
Client
NZI Insurance

Obviously, this sign was not insured with our Total Replacement House Policy
NZI Insurance
Peace of Mind
ON THE ROOF
IN BY 9:00 a.m.
$2.00
PER DAY

For Once, An Insurance Company
Is Glad To See Something Catch On Fire.
Proud Patron of U.S. Olympic Festival-'90.
The St Paul
COMPANIES
NAEGELE
TWIN CITIES

Creative Director
Bert Gardner
Art Director
Mike Gustafson
Design Agency
Bozell Inc., Minneapolis
Illustrator
Warren Hanson
Copywriter
Dick Thomas
Client
Saint Paul Companies

Up in the air about a loan? 341-RATE
first national bank of omaha
member FDIC
IMPERIAL

Creative Director
Frank Ervin
Designer
Frank Ervin
Design Agency
Bozell Inc., Omaha
Copywriter
Jeanette Bendtsen
Client
First National Bank of Omaha

Up in the air about a loan? 341-RATE
first national bank of omaha
IMPERIAL

Up in the air about a loan? 341-RATE
first national bank of omaha
IMPERIAL

Build Your Nest Egg
With Our "Better-Than-a-T-Bill" Account.
FIRST FEDERAL LAKEWOOD

Feather Your Nest
With A Home Improvement Loan.
FIRST FEDERAL LAKEWOOD

Feather Your Nest
With An I.R.A.
FIRST FEDERAL
LAKEWOOD

Tiered Investments
For Empty Nesters.
FIRST FEDERAL LAKEWOOD

Creative Director
Gerald Patno
Art Director/Designer
Denny Pavan
Design Agency
Belden Frenz Lehman, Westlake
Illustrator
Jerry Small
Copywriters
Denny Pavan, Gerald Patno
Client
First Federal of Lakewood

Art Director
Ken Woodard
Design Agency
Ketchum Advertising,
San Francisco
Copywriter
David Wolf
Client
Southwestern Bell
Yellow Pages

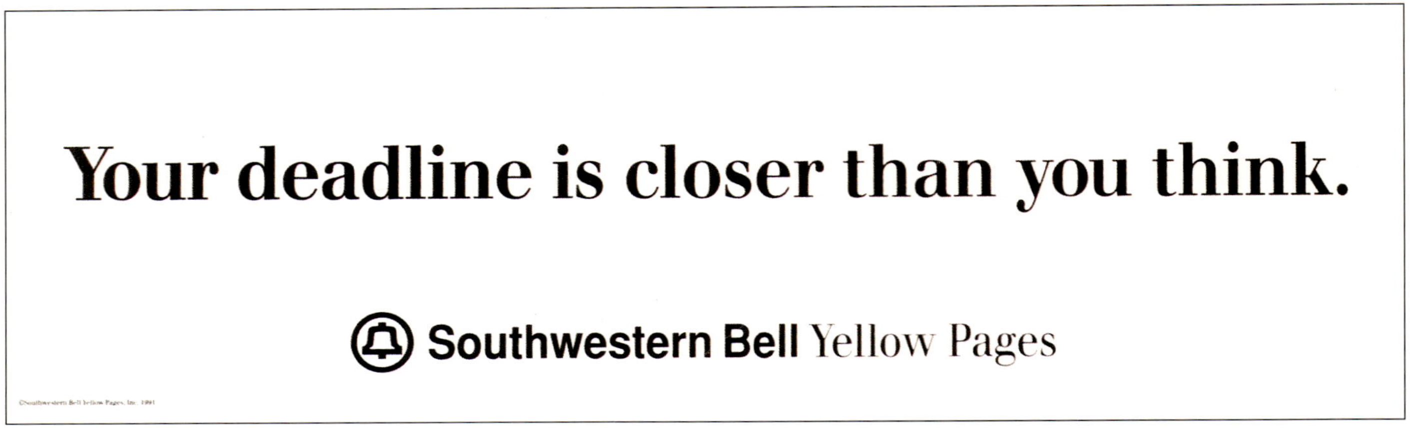
Your deadline is closer than you think.
Southwestern Bell Yellow Pages

Your deadline is closer than you think.
Southwestern Bell Yellow Pages

Your deadline is closer than you think.
Southwestern Bell Yellow Pages

Even he couldn't find a buried utility line.
Call 454-0002 before you dig.
NSP
NAEGELE

Art Director
Wayne Thompson
Design Agency
Martin/Williams Inc./
Edison Group,
Minneapolis
Illustrator
Jim Round
Copywriter
Steve Kurtz
Client
Northern States Power

The phone rings. You pick it up.
It's your roommate's ex-girlfriend complaining about why he dumped her.
The phone rings. You pick it up.
It's your roommate's current girlfriend complaining about things in general.
The phone rings. You refuse to pick it up.
And it's the goddess from Greek class who you thought only wanted a platonic relationship.
Smart Ring
GTE
THE POWER IS ON

She works at the library. You start returning overdue books.
She likes classical music. You scrape the heavy metal stickers off your bumper.
She's an Art major. You consider throwing away two years of Economics.
She actually calls you.
Your line is busy.
Call Waiting
GTE
FOR DETAILS CALL 1-800-843-2120 EXT 4142.
THE POWER IS ON

You've worshipped him from afar all semester.
You've heard his last girlfriend was blond. You bleach your hair.
You've enrolled in classes you hate just to be near him.
He finally calls.
Your line is busy.
Call Waiting
GTE
FOR DETAILS CALL 1-800-843-2120 EXT 4142.
THE POWER IS ON

Creative Directors
Rick Carpenter, Mark Monteiro, Jaci Sisson
Art Director
Patrick Arroff
Design Agency
DDB Needham Worldwide, Los Angeles
Photographer
Mathew Ralston
Copywriters
Perrin Lam, Debbie Fried
Client
GTE (General Telephone)

Motel M
Use it for ZZZZs.
The Yellow Pages
USWEST DIRECT

Weight Control W
Use it to lose it.
The Yellow Pages
USWEST DIRECT

Storage S
Use it to conquer space.
The Yellow Pages
USWEST DIRECT

Art Director
Andy Candelaria
Design Agency
Grey Advertising, Los Angeles
Photographer
Ken Sabatini
Copywriter
Jim Chase
Client
U.S. West Direct

GTE
7
For getting around town, nothing outperforms your phone.
GANNETT OUTDOOR
0889

Creative Director
Rick Carpenter
Art Director
Dennis Menarcy
Designer
Rick Carpenter
Design Agency
DDB Needham, Los Angeles
Photographer
Dennis Menarcy
Copywriter
Mark Monteiro
Client
GTE

GTE
For getting around town, nothing outperforms your phone.
0737
GANNETT OUTDOOR

Art Director
Garry Emery
Design Agency
Emery Vincent
Associates, Australia
Client
Southgate/Jennings
Group Limited

Art Director
Garry Emery
Design Agency
Emery Vincent
Associates, Australia
Architect
Robert Peck
Client
Sandridge City
Developments

Index of Creative Directors, Art Directors, Designers, Photographers, Illustrators and Writers